Bhor Moshe Sara
Notrica Notrica

MiRiAM
NotRiCA

Sara Victor
and Stella

AVID

READER

PRESS

ONE HUNDRED SATURDAYS

*Stella Levi and
the Search for
a Lost World*

MICHAEL FRANK

Avid Reader Press
New York   London   Toronto   Sydney   New Delhi

AVID READER PRESS
An Imprint of Simon & Schuster, Inc.
1230 Avenue of the Americas
New York, NY 10020

First Avid Reader Press hardcover edition September 2022

AVID READER PRESS and colophon
are trademarks of Simon & Schuster, Inc.

For information about special discounts for bulk purchases,
please contact Simon & Schuster Special Sales at 1-866-506-1949
or business@simonandschuster.com.

The Simon & Schuster Speakers Bureau can bring authors to your live event. For
more information or to book an event, contact the Simon & Schuster Speakers
Bureau at 1-866-248-3049 or visit our website at www.simonspeakers.com.

Interior design by Alex Kalman and What Studio?

Manufactured in the United States of America

1   3   5   7   9   10   8   6   4   2

Library of Congress Cataloging-in-Publication Data has been applied for.

ISBN 978-1-9821-6722-6
ISBN 978-1-9821-6724-0 (ebook)

"The tremendous world I have inside my head . . ."

—Kafka

The sea isn't wine-dark so much as a blue so bottomless and transparent that it hurts to look into it, the way it can hurt to look into another person's eyes. I am gazing at this bottomless, transparent blue and I am listening to a ninety-two-year-old woman describe what happened by its shore, at this spot where we are standing, seventy-one years ago nearly to the day.

July 23, 1944: A Sunday. The Germans deliberately chose a Sunday, she tells me, because on Sunday all the shops were closed. And they sounded the air-raid sirens, even though no planes flew overhead, even though no bombs fell out of the sky that day, because the sirens kept everyone indoors—everyone else. In all the hours—six, maybe more—that it took them, 1,650 of them, to walk down to the port, not a single civilian bore witness, or objected, or came to say good-bye.

It was like a funeral cortege, she says, of people in mourning for themselves.

At this spot where we are standing, the entire Jewish community of the island of Rhodes—her community, on her island, the place she considered her own little piece of the earth—was loaded onto three boats that would take these 1,650 human beings to the port at Piraeus, and from there to the prison at Haidari, and from there to the trains that would deliver them to Auschwitz two weeks later, cumulatively the longest journey, measured by time and geography, of any of the deportations and in many ways one of the most, if not *the* most, absurd.

"We were old people and young women and children," she says. "Most of us had never been off the island in our entire lives, and that included me. It would have been simpler to murder us all here and let us, at least, be buried with our own kind."

Now the ninety-two-year-old—Stella Levi—looks at the water, at the horizon. She stares at the clean, sharp line that separates water from sky, one blue from another. Then she turns back toward me. Her face is shadowed, her eyes remote, seeing what I am unable to imagine.

For a long moment she is silent. Then she says, "Maybe after a certain point you can no longer come back in person. Maybe you can only go back in your mind."

Stella has come, not for the first time but possibly the last, to the Juderia of Rhodes—to connect, or reconnect, or try to connect, once again, to the neighborhood in which she was born and grew up, like her parents and grandparents before her, and generations before them, all the way back to the late fifteenth century, when these Sephardic Jews were banished from Spain and scattered across Europe and the Mediterranean. Because she has come here, I have too, even though I don't yet know her even a fraction as well as I will. Having learned, while I was in Rome, that she was planning to make a late-in-life return visit to Rhodes, I booked a ticket and more or less invited myself. Later she will tell me this was one of the reasons why she decided to trust me with her story. Later I will understand that I went, in part, to earn her trust.

The two of us had met just a few months earlier at Casa Italiana, the Greenwich Village home of the Department of Italian Studies at NYU, where one evening in February 2015, late for a lecture, I hastily dropped into a chair, the only open seat remaining at a long rectangular wooden table. As I was catching my breath, a question came floating over my shoulder, posed in a thick Italian accent: "Where are you coming from that you're in such a hurry?"

The woman asking this question was older, elegant. Her features were emphatic, her hair tinted brown and immaculately shaped to frame her face. She was wearing a dark skirt, a cardigan, silver rings with stones on alternating long fingers.

I told her that I was coming from a French lesson. She nodded thoughtfully.

I had come to Casa Italiana, as she had, to listen to a talk about the relationship among museums, memory, and Nazi Fascism. The speakers would discuss memorials, the challenges of marking the actual settings where abhorrent events have taken place or of marking, or commemorating, these abhorrent events in unrelated places.

She had a second question now: "Might I ask *why* you are studying French?"

Her brown eyes were sharpened, honed with curiosity. I sensed her wanting, expecting, an incisive or at least an interesting answer. I only had the answer that I had. I explained that French was the first foreign language I ever learned, beginning in junior high school; after years of speaking more Italian, I told her, I was trying to bring it back. I didn't want to embarrass myself when I traveled, I said. I would like to read Proust in his own language one day.

Somehow, under her fierce gaze, I feared that all this came out as *baguette-croissant-beret*—as in, I would like to be able to ask for such items in a Parisian shop.

She nodded again. "Are you interested in knowing how French served me in my life?"

Having discovered that I spoke Italian, she switched languages, as now so did I. "*Certamente.*"

"When I arrived in Auschwitz," she said, "they didn't know what to do with us. Jews who don't speak Yiddish? What kind of Jews are those? Judeo-Spanish-speaking Sephardic Italian Jews from the island of Rhodes, I tried to explain, with no success. They asked us if we spoke German. No. Polish? No. French? 'Yes,' I said. 'French I speak . . .'"

She paused. "I spoke French, *some* French, because my sisters attended the Alliance Israélite Universelle. What they studied, they shared at home. Also I went on to study the language in school. Many of us girls from Rhodes did. Because we spoke French, at Auschwitz they put us with the French and Belgian women, who spoke French *and* Yiddish, and a little German too, enough so that they could translate and they could communicate. And they understood. Because they understood what was going on, they managed to survive—and therefore so did we."

She sat back in her chair. "*C'est comme ça que le français m'a servi dans ma vie.*"

• • •

The following morning, I received a call from Natalia Indrimi, the director of Centro Primo Levi, a New York–based organization dedicated to exploring the Italian Jewish past that had organized the lecture. I knew Natalia because I had asked her for help researching a story set in Italy during the war years, a subject that had interested me ever since I lived in Italy for a time in my twenties.

Stella Levi, Natalia said, the woman I'd sat next to the previous night, had enjoyed her visit with me. When I said that I had too, she went on to say that Stella had a little something she had written about her childhood and youth in Rhodes for a brief talk to give at one of Centro Primo Levi's upcoming evenings, and as she was unsure of her written English, she wondered if I would meet with her to help adjust those few pages.

Two days later, as I passed under a green awning on University Place, I had no way of knowing that this was the first of one hundred Saturdays spread out over the next six years that I would spend in the company of a woman I would come to think of as a Scheherazade, a witness, a conjurer, a time traveler who would invite me to travel with her.

Maybe you can only go back in your mind?
Maybe.

1

"For a while now I've been thinking it might be time for me to see a psychiatrist again."

This is nearly the first sentence Stella says to me when I step inside her apartment on Saturday.

"I don't know if a psychiatrist would even know what to do with me," she adds. "I went to see three in the 1950s, when I moved to New York. They didn't know what to do with me then either."

I haven't even stepped beyond her small foyer. I do now. Stella indicates a chair; I set my jacket onto it.

"They didn't know what to do with any of us who had come back from the camps. How could they, without having been there? Even when I told them, tried to tell them. But possibly *I* wasn't ready?"

Stella sits down in her armchair and points to the sofa arranged perpendicular to it. She is dressed in smart slacks, a white blouse, a different cardigan from the other night.

I sit down.

"What do you feel?" she asks. "Is it a good idea?"

I think: Psychotherapy—at the far end of life? Certainly it would take some researching, some trial and error, to find the right person. What would such a person be like? What would she have had to experience, or study, or read, to be able to understand, let alone help, someone who had lived through what Stella has?

She doesn't wait for me to respond. "I'm not sure. I haven't been feeling right—in myself. I guess what I really feel is the need to talk."

She looks at me head on, a ninety-two-year-old woman with a question, a need. Here we are: person to person, on a quiet Saturday afternoon in her home in Greenwich Village, meeting properly for the first time.

"Are the camps . . . something you want to talk about now?" I ask.

In her eyes a flash of feeling, not quite anger, but close. "I thought you came here to look at a few pages I've written about Rhodes."

"I have," I say carefully.

She gives me a look that I interpret as suspicious, then opens a folder. It turns out to be the wrong folder, so she springs up and heads toward her desk, which stands in a corner of the living room—and *springs* is the right word; it's as if a tightly wound coil is set free, sending her into the air.

I've never seen a ninety-year-old move like that. An eighty-year-old either, come to think of it.

A few seconds later she thrusts several typewritten pages into my hands. It's clear that she expects me to read and respond to them while I am sitting on this sofa, under her gaze. They feel like a test.

I read them carefully, aware of her eyes on me the whole time. In these pages Stella offers a snapshot, several snapshots, of her youth in the Juderia. She describes an exotic practice called an *enserradura*, something an older woman performed on you if you were a young woman, nearly always unmarried, and anxious or depressed: You were closed up in the house for seven or eight days with this older woman who was a kind of healer, a practitioner of folk remedies and cures—Stella's own grandmother, her mother's mother, was one. Confined for the entire week with this healer, all you were allowed to consume was water and a thin broth. Meanwhile, for the duration of the *enserradura*, the houses nearby on both sides were emptied out so that you could have complete silence and tranquility as this older woman sat by your bed holding a handful of *mumya*, which was said to be the ashes of Jewish saints brought back from the Holy Land. This older woman's hand, holding the *mumya*, circled your face while she said a prayer over you. She kept praying, and circling, until you yawned and she yawned, and then she started over again the following day. After seven or eight days, with a final yawn, you were deemed cured. You got up and went to the Turkish bath to wash and send all the bad feelings decisively away.

I finish reading about this practice, this *enserradura*, and look up at Stella, in the second decade of the twenty-first century, sitting in her living room, with its walls painted alternately deep ochre and a Pompeiian red, its shelves packed with books in five different languages, its floor

thick with muffling Turkish carpets, its computer, television, and devices.
"I'm going to guess you never had an *enserradura* performed on you when
you were a young girl."

"Oh? What makes you think that?"

"Intuition."

She focuses those biting, clear eyes of hers on me, then says, "Of
course not. I wasn't that kind of girl. None of my sisters was either. In fact
my sister Felicie—the intellectual in the family—used to say, 'We have to
stop even *speaking* about these things. Modernity has come—the West-
ern world is at our doorstep. Freud, Thomas Mann.'" She pauses. "*Now* I
can speak of them, though. Now I have come to see that the world I was
born into might have been . . . I don't know . . . interesting."

"You didn't think so then?"

"Then I wanted to be free. I wanted a life, a bigger life than I could
have in this small neighborhood on this small island in the middle of
nowhere."

She sits back, then indicates the pages I've just read. "So? How are
they?"

"Honestly, I'm not sure you need my help."

"The English isn't perfect," she says.

"The English isn't flawless, but the stories . . . the one about your
aunt, Tia Rachel, collecting rainwater on her terrace to wash her daughters' hair, standing outside with bowls and pans as the clouds open up
and rain comes sheeting down, and your uncle saying—"

"*Esta en ganeden*—she's in paradise."

When I seem confused, Stella adds, "It gave her such pleasure, you
see, to collect the rainwater." She makes a gesture with her hand. "I would
like you to fix up what I wrote. Will you?"

Yes, I tell her. I will.

2

In the intervening week I tinker with Stella's pages and send them to her by email. She writes back to say that she still feels they're all wrong. They're not, but as I will learn, it's not easy to satisfy Stella. Or, rather, it's not easy for Stella to be satisfied with herself.

I return the following Saturday, and we look over my suggestions. This takes us maybe ten, fifteen minutes in all. When we finish, she slips them back in her folder, gives the folder a melancholy glance, and sighs.

We sit together in silence.

I decide to say what I've been thinking during the past week. If she's game, I say, I would like to continue to come listen to her on Saturdays. I would like to ask her about her life, in Rhodes, and in the camps, and after the camps.

"Possibly the rest," she answers, "but not the camps."

"Why not the camps?"

"Because I don't want to be that person."

I ask her what she means. She describes the kind of survivor who has recounted her experience so often that it becomes atrophied, distant—mechanical; she doesn't see the point of people doing that. She has never wanted to be a performing survivor, a storyteller of the Holocaust, ossified, with no new thoughts or perspectives, and with this one event placed so central, too central, in a long, layered life.

I understand, I tell her. And yet—yet what if she began by talking to me about life in Rhodes *before*, along the lines of the pages she gave me to read? What if she could preserve those ways of living, those people, that world?

"There are just a handful of us left," she says thoughtfully.

"Another reason why," I say. "Because when you . . . go, the story of that place, and those lives, will go with you."

"You think I don't know that?" In a softer tone she adds, "There's so much I haven't told. Many parts, the—more difficult parts."

"Do you have any children?" I ask.

"One son, yes. John."

"Have you told those parts to John?"

"Only a few."

Why only a few, I wonder.

"I didn't want to burden him."

"And to your grandchildren, if there are any?"

"Three: Randy, Rita, and Lewis." She pauses. "And I have, a little, but . . ."

"But?"

"I wasn't ready, I suppose."

"Like with the psychiatrists?"

She doesn't nod. But she doesn't shake her head either.

"Are you ready now?"

"Maybe next time," she says. Then she stands up.

3

We resume our places the following Saturday: she in her armchair, I on the sofa next to a white porcelain lamp that is covered with three-dimensional flowers and leaves. We exchange pleasantries, then for one moment, and another, we sit in awkward silence.

"Aren't you supposed to ask me a question to get me going, like where I was born, or my first memory, or something like that?"

Those eyes: suspicious yet provoking at the same time.

"Why don't you tell me when you first knew you were different?"

"What makes you think I was different?" she asks, her eyes sparkling now.

She was fourteen, by a month or two. The notion came to her in the middle of the night—she had no idea how. Possibly from watching her just-older sister Renée turn sixteen and begin to spend hours sitting in their living room and their *kortijo*, the enclosed courtyard that was a feature of the better houses in the Juderia, all of a sudden like an adult woman bent over needlework at their mother's side, sewing, embroidering, preparing—for the husband she hadn't met, and wouldn't choose for herself. Nightgowns, handkerchiefs, table linens. Sheets, pillowcases. Stella despised all that handiwork.

She thought it was a ridiculous way for a girl to spend her time, preparing for this phantom man or boy that someone (her mother, another mother, an uncle, a matchmaker) was going to pluck from the available candidates and present to her like a prize. She had another idea. Before going to bed one night, she found an old suitcase in the back of a closet. She brushed away a thin coating of dust and spread the suitcase out on the floor. She packed it diligently, with clothes, shoes, empty notebooks, pens, a coat. She set it by the door, climbed in between her sheets, and went to sleep.

In the morning her mother found the suitcase and asked her if she was planning on going somewhere.

"Of course I am," she told her. "To university, in Italy."

"Of course, to university, in Italy"—Miriam, her mother, echoed. Miriam had not been educated beyond elementary school, and none of her daughters had gone beyond the equivalent of middle school except one. But she didn't laugh or become upset. She didn't say, *You might outgrow these clothes by the time you're eighteen.* She didn't say, *You'd be the first girl in the Juderia to do such a thing.* She simply nodded at the suitcase and let it be.

Perhaps it was easy to leave things be with the baby of the family, especially when there were the older girls, three left still to worry over and plan for, meaning to marry off and set up in life.

With Renée, the sister who was closest in age to Stella, it became a joke: Stella and her packed suitcase, Stella at fourteen prepared to go away to university in Italy. But not for Stella. She kept it ready for months, repacking it every so often. As the months turned into years, the jokes never went away. But neither did the suitcase.

4

Where *did* she get the idea to start packing, at fourteen, for university?

Possibly from her sister Felicie, though whether because of her or despite her, Stella can't decide.

They were seven siblings—Morris, Selma, Felicie, Sara, Victor, Renée, and Stella. But since Morris left Rhodes before Stella and Renée were born, and since Selma left when Stella was just six, for most of Stella's childhood Felicie was the reigning oldest child, and a very particular one at that.

Stella used to slip out of bed to listen to Felicie, who sat up late into the night with her friend Robert Cohen just to *talk*. Robert didn't seem to be Felicie's boyfriend. His socks didn't match, for one thing, and they sat far apart across the room from each other and never appeared to touch. But they spoke (and spoke . . . and spoke), exchanging ideas and mentioning names that Stella barely registered: Henri Bergson. Tolstoy. Proust. And Felicie didn't behave like other girls in the Juderia, or even in the family; she wasn't like Selma (what Stella remembered of Selma) or Sara, who helped their mother with the cooking. She sat in her room, reading, all day, all evening long. She didn't even come to dinner when she was called. She spent so much time reading that she developed a bald spot on the back of her head for which Dr. Hasson had to mix up a special *pomata*.

Felicie wasn't made for the modern world; she didn't belong in Rhodes. She had the brain of a European intellectual of the early 1900s in the body of a young woman who grew up in the Middle East; hers was a different mentality, a different way of being entirely. Felicie never cared about her clothes. She didn't bother to comb what little hair remained on the back of her head. When the family posed for a photograph just outside the medieval walls that enclosed the old city, she alone among the children turned her back to the photographer.

What was wrong with her? Was anything wrong with her?

5

Felicie was the first member of the family to leave the Juderia after middle school to be educated by the *suore*, the nuns, at the *scuola femminile*, the Italian high school for girls, thereby inspiring Stella to do the same. Felicie was such a memorably accomplished student that, years later, when it came Stella's turn to follow, the *madre superiora* greeted her the first day by saying, "*Vediamo un pò se sarai brava come Felicie*"—let's see if you turn out to be as good a student as Felicie.

Felicie set the standard. And not just at school. She and her like-minded friends took Stella to visit Monte Smith, where Italian archaeologists were excavating the acropolis, with its temples, stadium, and theater that was believed to have been used for a legendary school of Greek rhetoric. She visited Greek Orthodox churches too and liked to study the mosques—from the outside anyway. Felicie helped Stella to understand that they came from somewhere significant, somewhere with a wider horizon than the Juderia, the beach, and the Kay Ancha, the main piazza of the Juderia with its array of shops. Felicie was the first young woman Stella ever heard say that she had no interest in preparing her trousseau. She wouldn't even consider getting married; she had no boyfriend (or girlfriend); she challenged authority, precepts, assumptions.

Felicie explained human nature to her own parents. When Sara was out later than usual, and Miriam stood by the door, watching and worrying while Stella looked on, frightened for what might happen when she turned up, Felicie would sit down with her mother and father and deliver a mini discourse on human liberty and happiness to explain, and thereby justify, why it was perfectly fine for a young woman to exercise free will and come home whenever she chose. And surprisingly they would nod, absorb, agree—apparently agree.

It was from eavesdropping on Felicie, in her late-night talks with Robert Cohen, that Stella first heard anyone speak critically of the Fascist regime they had all grown up under, though at the time she scarcely understood what this meant. All she knew was that her older sister's conversation was somehow worrying to her parents, and if it had been overheard might have gotten all of them into trouble. "It's a good thing," Miriam said, "that they have their talks at night."

Felicie, the wise daughter, the reader, the clever student who was politically awake: she wrote a brilliant essay about crime and punishment in the thinking of the ancient Greeks that inspired David Amato, a rare member of the community who had gone abroad to further his studies, to propose that Felicie go to Paris, where she might attend the Sorbonne and train to become an educator, the obvious (and virtually the only) path for a bright young woman who was uninterested in marriage or working in a shop, an office, or at a trade.

Miriam had a cousin who lived in Paris. Felicie spoke French fluently. She would not be alone—there would be someone to put a bowl of soup in front of her and keep her company while she studied—but Felicie said no. Unhesitatingly, unequivocally no.

Stella took this hard, her sister's failure of courage: "Felicie was free, and free-spirited, in her mind but not, I discovered, in her soul. It would have changed her life, maybe all of our lives, who knows. But instead, my sister, she wouldn't even consider the idea; she was afraid of living in the outside world."

6

If Felicie was an imperfect model, Renée was the anti-model. Born in 1921, so two years older than Stella, Renée was fashionable; she was fastidious about every aspect of her clothing, her shoes, and her hair. Stella didn't care so much about how she looked (though she cared more than the plain-dressing Felicie). Renée was a *signorina*, a proper young lady, who never used words like the slightly coarse *pasticcio* (mess); Stella said whatever came to mind. Hesitant and delicate, Renée was diagnosed as an asthmatic, and attracted much of her mother's worry and coddling.

Stella was robust and eventually became a distance swimmer who set off for the beach in last season's hand-me-down bathing suit, whereas Renée had to have the newest style. Stella was an intrepid diver, she had dozens of friends. She was curious, ambitious, and bold. Renée was more selective and discerning, her prudent opposite in every way.

"But do you know," Stella says, "after all these years I'm not sure whether Renée was born delicate and careful or whether my mother simply treated her that way and so that was what she became. As I would eventually discover, deep down she was strong, but she was *considered* the frail one, always warned to wear a sweater, to avoid the water if it was too cold. That's how it is in families. One person is one way, the next must be different . . ."

I ask Stella what that left her with.

"The freedom to choose what I wanted to be," she says.

7

At fifteen, Renée set to work on that trousseau, she and Miriam together. There was nothing else for Miriam to do after the older girls had gone—and there was no trousseau-making for Felicie, certainly. She made Renée a beautiful *camicia da notte* of satin; she embroidered table linens and the borders of hand towels. Renée, as if on cue, turned sixteen and had *un flirt* with the son of Alhadeff the banker; there was talk in the community, and Miriam heard about it. As part of the far less well-to-do branch of a rich banking family, Miriam had an acute sense of the local social hierarchy. "Don't get above your station," she told Renée. "It will never happen." And it never did.

If Renée couldn't marry the banker's son, then whom *could* she marry?

Certainly no one in the family, even though cousins were known to marry in the Juderia. Stella's maternal grandmother, Sara Notrica, the healer, was among them. She'd been married to her first cousin Moshe

Notrica, and her verdict on that particular configuration was this: "*Never marry a relative, never ever.*"

The girls grew up hearing this all the time. It was a warning, a curse. When a cousin in Congo, a perfectly respectable young man, proposed to Renée, she said she couldn't even consider the idea.

Moshe Notrica died before she was born, but Stella grew up knowing that these cousin-grandparents of hers lived apart—in that time and in that place—and it made an impression on her. So too did the fact that her grandmother Sara lived in a house loaned to her by her wealthy banker brother Giuseppe Notrica, a notable philanthropist in the community who had no children of his own and was determined to improve the lives of young people (he endowed the school, built houses whose rent provided books and clothes for indigent students, and established the Fondazione Notrica, a social and cultural center that presented lectures and held dances and other entertainments for local youth). From early on Stella had a strong understanding that, on her mother's side anyway, her family belonged, yet didn't quite belong, to a certain class of people. "You never know in which direction the wheel of fortune will spin," Miriam pointedly told the girls. "It's best not to envy, or resent, what other people have."

Miriam may not have *openly* resented, but she acted in a way that told a more nuanced story. When she came to live with her mother-in-law in her house across the street from the synagogue, the Kahal Shalom, Miriam improved it by bringing with her the furniture that had been part of her trousseau: a credenza, a handsome table and chairs, wrought iron and gilded bedsteads that seemed too fine and too elegant for the setting as it stood. She installed marble on the living room walls; a pavement of black-and-white stones known as *sheshikos*, as was the style in the better homes in Rhodes; a crystal chandelier; and an entry with an attractive gate. "My father grumbled because he didn't like to spend money," Stella tells me, "but he had married a Notrica . . . and anyway he always gave my mother what she wanted."

He had married a Notrica, meaning a young woman who came from money but didn't necessarily have it herself. The Notricas, the Menasces, the Alhadeffs—or the branches of those families who had means, since not all of them did—had moved outside of the Juderia, to a neighborhood known as the Marash ("outside the city walls" in Turkish), large swaths of which had originally been a humble Greek quarter that the Italians rebuilt with modern houses fitted with bathrooms and state-of-the-art kitchens presided over by housekeepers in starched uniforms, not mothers or grandmothers. Stella would end up going to high school with some of the girls from the Marash, and despite her mother's *stated* philosophy, which she understood and tried to metabolize, she wasn't immune to feelings that certain inevitable comparisons brought on, especially after synagogue, or on holidays. "Our better-off relatives stopped by after services to take a sip of wine or taste one of Mamma's marzipans, but they never stayed for dinner. It may seem like a small thing, but children can be very sensitive to these differences, and it marked me. It marked me in ways I didn't understand until much later in life, when for too long a time I ended up caring too much for clothes, appearances, material goods . . ."

When Sara Notrica died, for seven mornings a chauffeur steered a gleaming black car into the narrow streets of the Juderia and delivered her well-to-do brother Chaim to the Levi house, so that he could sit and mourn and pray with the rest of the family; then every evening the chauffeur collected him again and whisked him off, it seemed, not to just another neighborhood but another world.

That too was something that marked Stella. That too she never forgot.

8

It's not as though the Levis were struggling, at least not in the prewar years. Stella's father was one of the more successful Rhodeslis (*Rhodeslis* is how people from the community refer to themselves in Judeo-Spanish); a supplier of wood and coal, he continued a business started by his father. He had a monopoly on government contracts for selling coal, with a territory that stretched to twelve islands, and with a Turkish partner he operated the all-important customs scale at the port. For decades the business thrived, and the family lived well, or well enough, not like the rich banker uncles but with sufficient resources to engage the services of a housekeeper, a laundress, and a woman who came to make *fideos*, Signora Rachel di Dalva, who gave Stella the job of hanging the angel-hair-like pasta out to dry on the railing that lined the terrace. With another family they also shared a festively painted two-room *cabina* on the beach, where the younger children spent much of their summers in joy-filled, sunlit freedom.

Nevertheless the Levis were very much in, and of, the Juderia, which is something that Stella absolutely does not regret, at least not now (it was a different story when she was sixteen, eighteen, twenty and bristled under some of the restrictions that came with being embedded in such a tight-knit community). During her childhood and youth on Rhodes, the Jews, the Greeks, and the Turks, and eventually the Italians too—despite their different backgrounds, religions, languages, and cultures—managed to share the island as they had for centuries in relative harmony, but nevertheless where one lived mattered deeply, and it has come to matter more and more to Stella as she has looked back over the abiding themes of her long and varied life: "When you lived outside of the Juderia you didn't truly belong, since it wasn't possible to belong, not truly, to the Italians, the Greeks, or the Turks."

By remaining in the Juderia, Stella tells me, you lived among the old women who sat outside and told stories in the afternoon within emergency oil-lamp-lighting, or prayer-saying, distance of the synagogue. You took your dishes to be baked in the communal oven and while you waited for them to finish baking you spent the hour gossiping with your friends. You didn't bathe at home because there were no baths at home, or showers either, but at the Turkish baths, once a week, before Shabbat. You sang and learned the Spanish *romansas*; you absorbed, and came to live by, the proverbs (twelve thousand counted by one scholar alone) as though they were molecules in the air or blood in your veins; you learned to prepare your grandmothers' sweet and savory dishes; you walked with care across the uneven cobblestones; and you fell asleep inhaling the perfume of the courtyards with their intense, unforgettable brew of jasmine and rosemary, lavender and roses and rue.

"None of the girls who *lived out* could tell you anything about any of this," Stella says. "But I can."

9

One evening when she was eleven or twelve, Stella was again listening to Felicie and Robert Cohen speak deep into the night, this time about God, but what, specifically about God, she wasn't certain—until the next morning when at breakfast their father, who had apparently also been listening, said to Felicie, "Did you and Robert mean to say that *man* invented *God*? Did I hear that right?" After taking a deep breath Felicie answered, "Yes, Papa, that's how I see it, that's how a lot of us see it nowadays."

Man invented *God*? Stella expected an earthquake, a tempest. Instead Yehuda's head fell to an angle. He wasn't offended; he was perplexed, curious. Confused. This man who, like most people in the Juderia, followed the Jewish religious calendar through the year, and who never missed a call to prayer, a holiday, or a ritual, and who always went off to work wearing his tzitzit, albeit hidden out of sight under his shirt, and who spent his sabbath afternoons after services reading the Talmud, merely took in what Felicie had to say. He respected her intellect; he believed she knew something, saw or possibly understood something that he did not—"Either that, or he didn't want to pick a fight."

For Stella it was the first time she heard anyone question (or examine, or reflect on) their religion. The Levis lived opposite the Kahal Shalom. Every time there was a fright or a concern, a piece of worrying or bad news, Miriam would send the girls flying across the street to say a prayer or light an oil lamp, or she would hurry there herself. The synagogue was their anchor; Judaism organized their time, their sense of the world, their consciousness—but did it have to?

10

Yom Kippur that fall was, as usual, preceded by one of Stella's least favorite rituals, the ceremony of kapparot, when family members stood still as a live, squawking chicken was circled around her (or his) head, with the belief that her (or his) sins would thereby be transferred to the chicken. A familiar phrase was recited, much and variously invoked in the Juderia, "*kon el nombre de Avraam, Yishak, i Yakov*"—in the name of Abraham, Isaac, and Jacob—and then the shochet slaughtered the chicken, which was afterward given to the poor.

When she was a small girl, sometimes Stella was lucky: because her family was so large, they ran out of chickens before it was her turn. But not this year. She closed her eyes, gritted her teeth . . . and soon the unpleasantness was over.

After the kapparot, they left Felicie, the nonbeliever, at home to read—she made a point, on this, the holiest day of the year, of at least reading the Bible, or Biblical commentary—while the rest of the family went across the street to the synagogue.

Stella took her place upstairs with the other women. About halfway through the service, she looked down as several of the men, among them her neighbor and good friend Nisso Cohen, stood up to approach the ark. Before these men stepped up onto the platform that stood before it, they shook off their slippers, as was their custom, being Cohanim, and at that moment Stella heard the word *Adonai* sung in a piercing, plangent voice and felt a chill travel through her entire body; she felt, briefly, as if she were levitating over her seat, no longer anchored in it but floating, weightless, there and not there at the same time. "I had no idea what this was or what this meant, I had never felt anything like it before and I never felt anything else similar until a lifetime later, when the nephew of my friend Fanny Levy brought back hashish from his honeymoon in Mexico, and I had a few puffs and, voilà, the same chill, the same floating"—and, with it, the awareness that she could neither name nor identify when she was a girl, but which she understood as an adult to be a recognition that the human brain, that spongy mass of fat and protein, had a most powerful, mysterious control over her consciousness and could suggest a sense of something higher or larger, something *beyond*.

"Is that the definition of belief, then, the sensation that you are rising up, that you are somewhere other, that some other possibility exists out there? That's what I experienced when I was a girl, just that once, only I didn't believe it was God that I was feeling then, and I didn't believe it was God when I smoked that hashish, and I don't believe it now, but I did feel *some*thing. And I remembered the feeling all my life."

11

The women in the family who remained unwaveringly devout were Stella's grandmothers.

For Stella's paternal grandmother, Mazaltov Levi, synagogue was the only place, other than the Turkish baths, and the cement bench outside of (and built into) the house, where she actually *went*. She had her fixed seat that she took most every Saturday morning; she knew the prayers and believed in their powers; the ritual gave shape to her week, her month, her life. A story was told about Mazaltov that illustrates how her religion formed her entire perspective: One day in the teens, when the first tourists began visiting Rhodes, a ship from Spain docked on the island. The travelers were accompanied on a guided visit to the Juderia, and Mazaltov, hearing these visitors speaking Spanish, declared, "But how wonderful, they're all Jews!"

Her grandmother believed that they were all Jews simply because they spoke Spanish, which was close enough to the language the Levis spoke at home: Judeo-Spanish, meaning the old Spanish—Castilian—that the banished Jews took with them when they left Spain, folding in over the centuries some Portuguese, a bit of Greek but more Turkish (which was logical given that it was the language of the longtime rulers of the island), and of course Hebrew. "Can you imagine the simplicity of a woman like that?"

I shake my head. Stella shakes her head.

"I'm not even sure that she ever once in her life stepped outside of the Juderia. In fact I don't think she ever did." Again Stella shakes her head. "We're talking about ten, twelve square blocks in all."

Her grandmother Sara was an entirely different story. She didn't merely leave the Juderia. Every year after a certain age, when she was in view of eighty, she traveled to Jerusalem, where she hoped to die and be buried, which in Rhodes and elsewhere in the Jewish Mediterranean was considered the most desirable place to end one's life. Her banker brother, Giuseppe, and his wife had gone there to do just that and eventually succeeded, but each time Sara went to Jerusalem, she kept on living. So she would fill her bags with *mumya* and other herbs and cures, come home to the island, and get back to work.

When she returned from her trips Sara would gather the grandchildren around and tell the story of her adventures, her visit to the tombs of Abraham and Sarah, say, where she walked down a narrow tunnel, following a flickering candle, and how it was frightening and beautiful, both at once. Arguably, though, this was less Sara the believer than Sara the storyteller who not only after her travels but often on winter evenings would enchant the children with *konsejas*, tales of an often moral or instructive or silly nature, like those that featured Joha, the wise fool, or foolish wise man, at any rate a memorable trickster who was much invoked in the Juderia of Stella's youth.

12

Sara was not a trickster and nor was she a fool; she was a wise woman, much in demand in the Juderia. "To have a grandmother like that," Stella says, "was a source of pride."

Picture this, she tells me—

Young women who succumbed to frequent spells of anxiety. Yehuda one winter catching a cold, a serious cold that progressed into pneumonia. In the uneven, unlit stone streets of the Juderia, people, young and old, robust and frail, afraid of falling and wounding themselves, or indeed falling and wounding themselves. Who did these struggling or suffering people turn to, what did they do, for cures and remedies, or to soothe and calm their nerves and fears?

Two Jewish doctors practiced in the Juderia, Dr. Hasson (Felicie's pomade-maker) and Dr. Gaon. Outside of the neighborhood a Greek physician, Dr. Filo, who spoke Judeo-Spanish, was occasionally consulted as well. The family dentist, also Greek, practiced fifteen minutes away on foot outside the walls. But often, before anyone ran to the professionals, they turned to the old women who'd received recipes and cures, practices and prayers, from their mothers and grandmothers and were constantly being summoned, hurrying from one house, one sickbed, to another.

Late in life, Stella's older cousin Rebecca Amato Levy—the daughter of Rachel who washed her daughters' hair with rainwater—wrote a book of personal reflections called *I Remember Rhodes*. Stella lifts it off her shelf and reads me her cousin's description of following their mutual grandmother into the homes she was requested to visit:

> With an air of confidence, she would enter the home of the sick as if she were a doctor. Her carriage was regal. She wore a long gown and robe (*sayo* and *antari*), a small hat (*tokado*) with the brooch in the center of her hat, and a gold belt and necklace.

Her first words upon entering the home were '*traimi un
punado de sal!*' Bring me a fistful of salt.

Stella's eyes gleam as she tells me that the *enserradura* was simply the
most extreme, and longest, of these treatments and maybe for that reason
the one that remains especially vivid to her—either that, or maybe because whenever it was being administered in her street she and her sisters
were sent to sleep over at their cousin Sara's and stayed up late into the
night playing, a mini holiday.

There were other cures, though, ones that Stella observed for herself
and ones she learned about later on, because by the time she came of age
they were beginning to fade away:

For falls, if you were a child, or for night fears or bad dreams experienced at any age, the old woman would calm you down by applying three
pinches of sugar on your tongue, and she would recite *Kon el nombre del
Dyo* or *Kon el nombre de Avraam, Yishak, i Yakov*. Sometimes, as a kind of
reprimand to the street that caused you to fall or injure yourself, the old
woman would ask you to accompany her to the exact spot where the mis-
hap took place, and she would throw salt or sugar down on the ground
and recite the prayer. Stella saw her grandmother do this frequently.

Salt served many purposes. It could play a role in the *enserradura* (in
combination with, or in lieu of, *mumya* if the latter was scarce), and even
outside of the *enserradura* the old women would take a few pinches in
their hands and circle your face—a practice known as a *prekante*—if you
had been frightened (for example, if you'd seen a rat, or if you walked all
of a sudden into a dark, scary room, like an attic or a cellar).

To cure acne, leeches were applied behind each ear. Stella vividly
remembers watching as her older sister Sara underwent such treatment:
Miriam picked up one leech, which kept creeping off course and crawling
down Sara's neck, and put it back where it belonged.

To ease the severe asthma—much more severe than Renée's—that
afflicted their aunt Lea Galante Notrica, the suffering woman was made
to tent her head with a towel over a basin filled with marijuana smoke
and inhale, or else drink a tisane brewed from the same herb.

To resolve Stella's father's cold, the one that progressed into pneumonia, Stella's grandmother Sara treated him with *las ventozas*, or cupping: a wick was lit, dropped into a glass, and the glass was upended on his back, where the rising heat created suction that was believed to draw the toxins out of the body. Sometimes the skin reacted—puffed up too high—in which case tiny incisions were made with a knife to cause it to deflate again.

For *sarampion*—measles—a specialist came in, a Turkish man who accompanied you to the beach, where he washed you down with cold seawater. For more severe cases he also made little slices in your forehead.

For fainting fits or dizzy spells, lemon was often inhaled.

For Miriam's *dolores de kavesa*, likely migraines, Sara treated them in this way: she sliced lemons or potatoes extra thin, placed them on Miriam's forehead, and wrapped her head with a tight cloth. Potatoes were also effective at absorbing fever; after they'd been wrapped around a burning head and left there for some time, they were practically cooked.

"My God," I say to Stella when she tells me that one.

"Don't say, 'My God,' Michael. There was a logic to these cures. They had been handed down through the generations. And, what's more, they worked."

13

When I arrive the following week, Stella's cousin's book is still on the table in front of me. While Stella is filling her water glass, I open it.

For *bukeras*, or sores on the corners of the mouth, you are to rub them early in the morning against anything made of steel still covered in dew.

For symptoms associated with having had an encounter with the evil eye (*oju malo* in Judeo-Spanish), such as loss of appetite, lethargy, and so on, you are to wear a blue stone or bead. Or throw a handful of salt into the toilet while urinating. (Salt again!)

These stone beads, Stella tells me when she sits down, or their near relations, a charm in the form of the hand of Fatima, she and her sisters often wore pinned to their underclothes (sometimes along with sprigs of *ruda*, or rue) as an insurance against all kinds of worries or dangers or hurts.

For *los locos*, the mentally disturbed: there was nothing to be done. After the Italians took charge, such people were sent to an institution in Palermo, and for years afterward Palermo was associated with mental illness. If someone displayed behavior that was *loko* or even just *un poko loko* people would ask, "*Mandaremos a Palermo?*"—Shall we send him to Palermo?

For festering sores, rheumatism, or arthritis: A crosscut was made on the arm or leg, and a garbanzo bean was placed in the middle of the incision, covered with a grape leaf (*oja de kura*), and held in place with a knotted scarf. After a few days, a sore would appear, the leaf would be changed, and also the bandage, which would be filled with pus from the sore that developed. This continued until the pain, and the toxins causing it, went away.

(This time I refrain from uttering "My God." I know better by now.)

For *gota*, a stroke, there was no cure at all.

I flip ahead in Rebecca Amato Levi's book to a collection of folk beliefs, and begin rapidly taking notes—

> *You do not borrow eggs at night*
> *You do not talk about teeth at night*
> *A bed without a pillow is bad luck*
> *If you are speaking about death and you sneeze, you must*
>   *pull your earlobe*
> *If you eat at the table without a tablecloth, the devil will*
>   *come and put you down as a tablecloth*

The list is long, compelling, in places dreadful. But to Stella's mind what's truly interesting is the *why* behind these beliefs:

The salt or sugar being thrown down into the street where people fell, or were afraid to fall, and the prayer being recited afterward? This, Stella points out, is connected to the topography of the Juderia and its history. Before the Italians came, before there was electricity, after nightfall the narrow streets of the Juderia were indeed verifiably dangerous, and people were afraid of falling and not being found until morning, so someone devised a response using the tools at hand (salt, sugar, a prayer).

The bed without a pillow? That was because when someone died, it was customary to take the pillow away. Stella's father, after sitting beside her grandmother Mazaltov's deathbed, at one point eased the pillow out from under his mother's head. Everyone understood what that meant.

After I close the book, Stella reminds me that the Rhodes of her youth was undergoing a multifaceted transition toward modernity. While her grandmothers' generation was still alive, yes, they continued to respect their beliefs and embrace their treatments, but even then there was an understanding that other choices, other ways, might be called for.

By the time her grandmothers had both died in the mid-1930s, everything had changed. "We let go of the old ways—well, *many* of the old ways. We went to the medical doctors more often. Anyway one or another of us was always running to the pharmacy—Menasce or Spano, we patronized both—for Veramon, the analgesic my mother took for her headaches, and other medicines that the pharmacists, as was the habit then, mixed up themselves. After all, you couldn't always count on there being a cold potato or a cucumber in the house when you needed it, could you?"

14

What about her mother, I ask Stella. Did Miriam have these healing skills—did they transmit from her mother and *her* grandmother?

Stella stands up, walks across the room, and picks up a framed photograph of a woman with crimped hair wearing an elegant dress, long necklaces, smart shoes. "Does a woman who dresses like this look like she might perform an *enserradura*?" she asks. Miriam was chic, clearly, and also, Stella adds, in many ways modern in her behavior and her thinking—certainly light-years more modern than *her* mother. But the truth is that she didn't have the time to run around and recite incantations over people when she had the house to run, the children to feed. This was her job, and with seven children it was nearly all-consuming for many years.

Like most of the women of her class in the Juderia, Miriam didn't do the food shopping; it wasn't considered proper for a lady to trade with (male) shopkeepers and tote her purchases around on her arm. Either the food came to her, from Turkish or Greek farmers or dairymen who visited the Juderia daily, or she sent the children to pick up what was needed. In fact Miriam only ventured into a shop to buy fabric to take to the dressmaker, or to the shoemaker to be fitted for—always—custom shoes. (The children in the next generation wore factory-made shoes imported from Italy.) Eventually a Turkish fellow called Gabai opened a tiny but convenient grocery store across the street from the Levis' house, but even then, if Miriam required something, she would still send one of the children, she never went herself.

Preparing the food was a different story. Miriam cooked, assisted by the older girls, Selma and Sara, while they were still at home, with Selma ending up being the most accomplished of all of them in the kitchen. Felicie pitched in—"so she wouldn't feel bad, and after all you can't read *all* the time"—but Renée and Stella, in the early years, were too young to lend a hand; instead they were given pieces of dough to play with.

Food prepared at home, as opposed to being sent to the communal oven, was cooked, typically, on two coal-fueled burners in the kitchen, though for larger meals and holidays Miriam would set up a kind of barbecue, also coal-fueled, in the *kortijo*. (Hot coals also provided the source of heat in the charcoal box irons they used to iron their linens.) Their diet was prepared on a base of olive oil; no one used butter, Stella says, until the Italians came, and never at all in the Levi home. When I ask Stella how she knows when butter was introduced, since that happened before she was born, and especially since it never appeared in her family's kitchen, she gives me the same answer she gives whenever I ask how she can know about something that happened in the earlier years of the twentieth century: "In my house everything was *told*. That's what you did on a Saturday evening: you told stories, you sang songs. The stories and the music, the *information*, became a thread that ran through the rest of my life."

Meals were divided into those made fresh and eaten that evening and those made ahead of time to eat on Saturday. The sabbath meal on Friday night was the most substantial dinner of the week, and typically included fresh fish or chicken. Saturday lunch was prepared on Friday but kept warm in a brazier and might be filled out with *burekas*, savory pastries with a variety of different fillings (meat, potato, spinach).

Vegetables were the foundation of their diet and were often enhanced with a bone or bit of leftover meat: eggplant, artichokes (in season), spinach, and *bamya* (okra; the secret was lots of lemon).

Other typical everyday dishes in the Levi house, and the community generally, included *pastels* or *pastelikus*, small, round meat-and-rice-filled tarts; *hojaldres*, a flatter, triangular version; and *boyus*, yet another, round form of filled savory pastry. All of these shapes could envelop fillings of meat or cheese (never together) or vegetables, with eggs often serving to bind the ingredients.

Dessert was serious business. The family ate so many sweets, Stella remarks, they should *all* have been diabetic, not just her father. Apricots, pears, apples, oranges, figs, and dates were combined in various pastry shapes with almonds or almond paste, walnuts, sesame, honey, cinnamon, and cloves, or else were candied. If candied, they were eaten with forks or spoons that stood at the ready in a *kucharera*, a special serving piece made of silver that included a receptacle for water to rinse the serving implement between uses. It was a common object in many households in the Juderia.

"And your mother made this, some version of all of this, every day?"

"*Most* every day," Stella says. "Yes."

15

What about wine, I wonder the following Saturday. Did her family drink much, or at all?

Rhodes was one of the first Greek islands to cultivate grapes and as early as the seventh century BCE was one of the biggest exporters of wine—amphoras from the island were found throughout the Mediterranean basin, recognizable because of their marks, either a rose or an image of Helios, the sun god. But the Levis were not great drinkers, no, perhaps a glass on Friday nights with the blessing and on holidays like Passover, and maybe now and then, if a guest came to dinner, a sip of ouzo ("diluted in water, of course"), but they did, it turns out, have a number of longstanding connections to wine and wine-making.

When Stella got her first period and was in pain, Tia Rachel told her to go see her great-uncle Yehuda Notrica. In his basement he distilled a strong libation into dark, mysterious bottles, a kind of cognac that took away the discomfort and put her instantly to sleep. Her great-uncle's cognac-making skills originated with his father, Stella's great-grandfather Behor Masliah Notrica, who owned several acres of vineyards near the village of Soroni, where Miriam's close relationship with a Greek family, Mihali Elias and his three daughters, continued through the generations, even after the vineyards were sold. "I will always remember how my mother's mood lightened, how she delighted in our visits to the village, where the Eliases baked bread with an egg inside, which became cooked along with the dough."

The Levis didn't eat their Greek friends' food, as it wasn't kosher; instead they brought their own and picnicked among the vineyards on fruit and cheese, olives and tomatoes (and the bread, which was permitted). On Assumption Day they attended the Panagia festival, an example of how this friendship casually expressed the cross-cultural openness that was typical of Rhodes and was echoed in a later relationship that Stella and Renée would develop with a different Greek family, Despola

Papathanasis and her brothers Mihali and Yoti, who attended the Italian school and became some of their closest friends.

"Drink, and food, originally connected us to these Greek people," Stella tells me. "But despite our coming from such different worlds, the friendships took hold and lasted all the way until the deportation."

16

The next Saturday Stella circles back to Renée. Another way the two differed: Stella was always going, seeing, doing. She loved to sleep over at her friends' and cousins' homes. Renée, instead, needed her bed, her soft pillow, her nightgown with its embroidered collar. Stella liked hanging out with the other kids; it was like a giant slumber party. All her mother cared about was whether she'd slept. "Of course, Mamma," she'd say, even if she hadn't.

One of Stella's favorite places to spend the night was across the street at Nisso Cohen's house, where she would often stay for days at a time. In the early mornings they would be awakened by the shamash of the synagogue as he summoned people to prayer by hurrying through the streets calling, "*La tefila, la tefila!*" while banging a stick on the iron bars on the windows.

"I can still hear that sound," Stella tells me. "I can still see that little man hurrying, hurrying . . ."

The Juderia was such an *alive* place. It was alive with scent, color, taste, movement, sound—so much sound, for so many hours of the day. When Stella wasn't sleeping over at Nisso's house she would often be awakened even earlier, by the first call to prayer in the morning, which boomed out from the minaret that towered over the mosque nearby. If she drifted back to sleep, and even if she didn't, the next thing Stella would hear was the gurgle of coffee being put up downstairs, which quickly followed by the whisking and mixing and kneading and banging about that started as her mother, or her neighbors' mothers, with all their windows and doors flung open to the bright morning light, would get an early start on the day's cooking. Next came the housemaids—for those who had them—who while they worked would sing to, and with, one another across the *kortijos* in Judeo-Spanish ("*De las altas mares . . .*") in a call-and-response that seemed to stand outside of time. As the morning advanced, along came the broom-maker hawking his wares, the Turkish vendors with the vegetables and their yogurt. Then the mothers, taking a break from their cooking, would call out, "*Ermana Touriel, sta ben oy?*" or "*Ermana Alhadeff, oy ke va azer?*" Next: the men reciting the morning prayers from the courtyard of the synagogue. After that, and threaded all through the day, singing: as children walked to school and back, as babies were put down for their naps, as young people gathered, and as women cooked or, later, as they embroidered deep into the night.

One morning, after a sleepover at Nisso's house, his father, Tio Jacov, was unwell, and Nisso asked Stella to help take him to the Italian hospital, in part because Stella's Italian was excellent. "We went by carriage—yes, with horses. The *carrozza* belonged to Colombo. You could have called a taxi, but that would have meant going a few streets farther along, and Colombo had his carriages nearby, and we all took them, my mother took them when she wanted to go to the Turkish baths like a lady . . ."

By carriage they went to see Dottore Galina, who examined Tio Jacov and said, "There's nothing to be done for this man. He has a fatal cancer."

Stella had never heard these words, or words like these, said of anyone she knew, or loved.

Not long afterward, she went to visit Tio Jacov. She walked into the room, the same room where she had her sleepovers with Nisso, the one with the iron bars against which the shamash made his sounds, and Tio Jacov looked at her, turned his head away, and went very still. It was the first time Stella had ever seen a man die, or a dead body.

She ran to tell his wife to stop doing the laundry because it was forbidden, she knew, to do the laundry when someone had died. Then she ran to tell her father to say the *Shema*.

"But, Stella, how do you know he's dead?" her father asked her. "How could you tell?"

She could tell, she told her father, because she saw him take his last breath.

17

Death: it terrified Stella when she was little. And for the longest time she was able to locate much of her fear in one place, in one man: the mortician Mazal, whose name, ironically, meant luck. He ran his enterprise out of a shop that was well stocked with coffins in different shapes and sizes despite the fact that most people who lived in the Juderia were buried in simple shrouds. Stella conjectures now that the coffins were used, essentially loaned out, to carry the body to the cemetery, then taken back to be aired and wiped down, recycled for the next unfortunate soul.

Stella was afraid to walk by Mazal's shop—all the girls (and a number of the boys) were. They never walked by; they always ran, often screaming.

They couldn't avoid his shop, because it stood in the Calleja de la Chavurah, one of the most important streets in the Juderia, also possibly one of the oldest, likely laid down before, possibly long before, the Knights came. The Knights: of St. John, also known as the Hospitallers, took control of the island in 1309, leaving a stamp on the cityscape that is still evident on the building stock of old Rhodes. They were preceded by the Persians, the Greeks, the Romans, the Genoese, and the Byzantines, and were followed by the Turks, the Italians, and the Germans. (Rhodes was a much conquered, much contested island, yet the Jews seem to have lived there, on and off, from time immemorial: in Genesis the people of Rhodes are described as descending from the grandsons of Noah.)

The very name of this narrow street gives a clue, Stella says, to what likely went on there ever since it was laid down. The Talmud uses the term *chavurah* to refer to a group of people who, in the days of the Temple in Jerusalem, gathered to perform the Pesach sacrifice; eventually the term came to describe a group ritual involving communal experiences that was held outside of the synagogue.

The communal experiences that took place in this street over the centuries hit pretty much all the fundamentals: education, religion, food . . . and death.

At one end of the Calleja de la Chavurah stood the Talmud Torah school that was in use when Stella's father was a boy; it occupied a building donated by the Camondo banking family. Down the road was one of the two ovens in the neighborhood where the matzah was baked every year for Passover and, the rest of the time, people would take their bread or pastries to be baked or dishes to be cooked. This meant that a tribe of young people, Stella often among them, would end up sitting outside the bakery in a large *kortijo* ringed with those built-in stone benches that were characteristic of the neighborhood, and they would sing or gossip or flirt: it was the teen hangout of the Juderia in the early decades of the twentieth century and, very likely, long before.

In this same street was the genizah, the place where Miriam sent Stella to deposit damaged or crumbling old prayer books through a little window. There they would remain until the time came, every few years or so, when the rabbi's assistant would collect all this printed matter—which had been carefully set aside in the event it had the name of God on it—and carry it to the cemetery to be buried.

But Mazal . . . Mazal was the centerpiece of the street—and more than just the street. It would have been one thing if he always stayed closed up in his terrifying shop, but this man was on the move and often, because it also fell to him to lead funeral processions through the Juderia. "*Pasa la misva!*" he called out as he approached. "*Pasa la misva!*" "If you were in the street, you ran in the opposite direction, or you darted into a house that wasn't your own. And if you were at home, you closed any windows that looked out onto the street and you backed away from the front door by a minimum of three feet—everyone, not just the children. '*Presto, presto, pasa la misva, pasa la misva.*'"

The funeral procession is known as a *misva* because it was considered a good (or moral) deed to accompany the dead to their final resting place.

Since it was obligatory for all funeral corteges to walk by a synagogue, and since the Kahal Shalom stood just a few steps from where the Levis lived, a lot of backing away from the front door—from death—went on in Stella's home when she was a little girl.

18

Stella's own experience of the rituals of death was very limited because women never attended a funeral, and if women never went, of course girls didn't either. "But that didn't stop me, especially after Tio Jacov died, from wanting to know more, *needing* to know more . . ."

Once the *misva* passed by the synagogue, it was off to the cemetery, where the men, after they said the prayers and saw the body lowered into the ground, washed their hands at a fountain that stood at the entrance, afterward carefully allowing them to dry by air. (The washing was to prevent negative spirits from attaching to the mourner's hands, and by air-drying them they were resisting the inclination to wipe away thoughts of sadness and loss.)

Stella knows more about what happened at home, because this she was able to observe firsthand: How a pitcher of water was left by the door, so that visitors could wash their hands before paying a condolence call, while paradoxically the chief mourners were not allowed to bathe or trim their fingernails for seven days. How everyone sat on cushions or carpets, but not the furniture, during that week of shivah, and wore torn.clothes for a month. How they were not allowed to eat their own food on the first day, only meals delivered by family and friends. How the first thing they *did* eat after a funeral was always a whole hard-boiled egg, a custom that continued long after the Juderia was no more: after Renée died in 2000, in faraway Berkeley, Selma emerged from the kitchen carrying a plate of hard-boiled eggs, still warm and in their shells.

At the time of a death and later, when death was discussed, invoked maybe too much or too deeply, possibly too upsettingly, many of these

Rhodeslis continued, for the rest of their own lives, to utter the phrase *"Leshos de mosotros"* (Far from us) or *"Guadrados de todo mal"* (May we be protected from all evil), just two of the hundreds of these near-incantations by which they once navigated, and protected, and understood, their lives.

As for the women, well, they grieved privately and without public ritual, with one exception that Stella has never forgotten, an age-old custom that disappeared with the death of her grandmother Sara, in fact possibly on that very day. As people began gathering for shivah, Tia Rachel, Sara's daughter and oldest child, the one who looked after her at the end of her life, started to go outside to produce *los lloros* to show the world how heartsick she was. It was the habit in the Juderia, following a death, for the women to step into the street (or, on certain occasions, to hire other women to go in their place) to wail or keen in public. *Los lloros*: the ultimate demonstration, and proclamation, of grief.

Poor Tia Rachel, she barely made it through the door before her brother Mazliah leapt to his feet and brought her back inside: "On her face there was such confusion, such . . . *shame.*"

Sara Notrica, the sister of Giuseppe Notrica, the banker and benefactor, was being mourned by the Alhadeffs and the Menasces, a more worldly, refined class of people, and it was too old-fashioned, it wasn't fitting, it was almost unseemly, Mazliah whispered, to have the dead woman's daughter standing outside, ululating in public. "Not today," Mazliah told his sister. "We've moved beyond this sort of thing now."

Tia Rachel turned around and sat down, quietly humiliated, and that was the end of *los lloros* in Stella's family, maybe in the whole of the Juderia.

19

Death woke Stella up, it grew her up—but death was by no means the only kind of loss she knew as a young girl.

She was born into a family with an absence: her older brother Morris, who at the age of ten had left for America with his aunt and uncle. He was a phantom, and he left a hole in the family, and in his mother's heart.

As Stella tells me about Morris, it strikes me that, between his leaving in 1920, before she and Renée were born, and the deportation in 1944, her nuclear family never once existed as a complete unit under one roof. No photograph exists of them together, no memory either, or single unifying story.

Such leave-takings continued all through Stella's childhood and beyond, into her young adulthood. After Morris, the next, and most heartrending, was Selma's. One winter a man from Rhodes returned to the island from New York, summoned by a matchmaker. The intended candidate turned him down. Selma was offered as a substitute: "When she saw him, she gasped." Stella taps her hand against her shoulder. "He came up to here, and my sister, well, she was a *giant.*"

The betrothal went ahead nevertheless.

The night before she left for her new life in New York, Selma insisted on sleeping in the same bed with Renée and Stella, her two baby sisters tucked alongside of her like puppies, one front, one back. They were eight and six, and no one slept because everyone held so tight and cried so long. They cried so much, in fact, that Miriam came in to say, "Daughter, you are taking a long trip tomorrow, you need your rest, you must stop all this crying."

How they fell asleep, Stella cannot say. In the morning Selma was gone.

Selma left in 1930. Six years later Sara followed. Selma was lonely and didn't care for her in-laws, the younger children were told; she needed her sister, she needed family nearby.

It was the sort of explanation you gave a child, but the truth was more complicated. The Levi children were following a long line of young people—men for the most part initially, but in time women too—who began to leave Rhodes near the turn of the century and continued after the Italians took control of the island and the local economy underwent a succession of downturns that included the failure of small family-run banks and businesses in the Juderia. This emigration continued until the promulgation of the racial laws in 1938 and afterward. Young men established beachheads that often turned into thriving businesses in the Belgian Congo, with variations on the theme in Buenos Aires, Cape Town, Rhodesia, New York, Los Angeles, and Seattle. Sending a son to these far-flung places, or a daughter (to marry these men), could easily mean not seeing them for years or decades or, in some cases, actually in many cases, ever again.

Stella remembers tears too when her older brother Victor left for the Belgian Congo in 1939. Miriam cried as she helped her son pack his bags, she cried into the night, and she cried the next morning as she and Yehuda blessed him at the door, as was customary, touching first the mezuzah and then Victor's head and saying a prayer before sending him off with a phrase: "*Ke tenga viajes buenos i kon mazal bueno*"—may you have a safe voyage and good luck.

The family was thinning. The young girls were growing up, taking the place of the older children. There were fewer chairs at the table, more empty beds—soon more expectations, and needs, would follow.

By the time Felicie left in 1940, on the last steamship to depart from Rhodes, traveling via Naples to New York and eventually the West Coast, the atmosphere in the Juderia had changed. The tears were more restrained, the feelings more ambivalent: "Looking back—it was almost as if my parents understood, or intuited, that Felicie would never have been able to survive what was about to happen to us. Of course, this is impossible since they had no idea what was coming. Maybe it was the mere *threat* of an uncertain future that convinced them that Felicie, being the most particular of us, should go. Also of course, she was the oldest one remaining, so her turn came next."

20

The sister Stella most physically resembled was Sara, who was known in the Juderia as a *kayijera*—someone who is seldom at home, always spending her time out and about in the streets (*kayes*, the likely origin of the word, in Judeo-Spanish), going, doing, partying. Stella was still too young to be a true *kayijera*, but she did, again in contrast to Renée, like to see her friends. A lot.

One afternoon she went to visit her friend and classmate Marie Menashe, who had the grippe and was in bed. Stella had heard that she wasn't taking her medicine, so she went to encourage her to, so that she might get better.

Stella was sitting on the second bed in her room, doing her best to convince the stubborn Marie to be sensible, when Marie's older brother Davide came in and sat next to her. Their two arms touched, casually touched, with no intention, no motive. He didn't sit next to Stella on purpose; it was just the obvious place to perch. He was nice-looking, though she had never thought of him, or any other boy, in *that* way.

"He sat down, our arms touched, and I felt a *frisson*, the first time I had ever felt such a thing for another human being. You know what a *frisson* is, Michael? *Un frisson sensuel?*"

"Yes, Stella, I know what a *frisson sensuel* is."

She extends her arm, touches it in the place where his arm touched hers. "I can still feel it."

She was twelve. That was more than eight decades ago. Yet she still remembers the feeling.

"It was the first time I sat down so close to a boy. Maybe at the beach you wrestle, you joke around, play at fighting in the sand or splash each other in the water, but I had never felt anything similar before. Not like this."

If that was Stella's first awareness, I ask her, how did she learn about . . .

"Not from my parents, *o Dio santissimo*, no. I never even saw them undressed. Even at the Turkish bath my mother was always covered. We girls were different."

"Did you ever see your parents touch?"

She shakes her head. "Never. Or hug, or kiss either. I never even saw them go out together. The only place they spent any time alone together was in bed."

They had seven children, I point out.

"Yes, but without ever explaining *how*. What I learned about that sort of thing I learned later from my sisters and my friends. And from books. We read a lot in the Juderia, you know."

21

All "that sort of thing" began in a small way with a gift that Selma sent Stella from New York: a two-piece floral beach cover-up that consisted of short pants and a top, which she put on with excitement whenever it was time to go to or come from the beach, even if she was only slipping up to the Italian café. With great pride she told everyone who asked, and anyone who didn't, that her sister had sent her the outfit from *Ah-merica*.

It surprised her that an outfit could change the way she thought about her body, and herself.

She was eight, maybe nine when the beach cover-up arrived, but older (fifteen, maybe sixteen) when Selma sent her another memorable gift, a beautiful yellow jersey dress, striped, that stood out against her dark tanned skin of summer. "*Signorina crema e cioccolato*," the Italian boys called her. Miss cream and chocolate. Her mother disapproved—not of the nickname, but the tan. She thought girls should protect their skin by avoiding the sun.

Did any of these boys become her boy*friends*?

She makes a clicking sound. Not these boys. Not yet.

Which boys? When?

"I'm not ready to tell you about that," she says.

• • •

Another reason Selma's first outfit was so memorable was that it was readymade. No one bought readymade clothing in the Juderia of Stella's youth, except possibly a sweater now and then or those imported shoes (and, in any event, only the young people), and that only began after the Italians were well established on the island. In the early years of Stella's childhood, after stepping into that one fabric shop, Miriam took her purchases to Josef Ben Attar, a tailor who came from Alexandria and dressed in a djellaba. Josef had a workshop with young apprentices, and he made Miriam's and the girls' dresses until eventually the Levis branched out to Stella's Notrica cousins, who sewed well and were family besides.

The patterns, the language of fashion, came from French magazines: *diagonalment, plissé, drapé.* Magazines had styles for *madame* and styles for *mademoiselle*—"We *never* overlapped"—and everyone at the very least always had a new dress for Passover and another for Rosh Hashanah.

Yehuda's clothes were also made for him, but by a Greek tailor who came to measure and fit him in the privacy of home. Like Josef the tailor, Yehuda wore a djellaba, striped and of good material, but only at home, never outdoors. He also, in the early years of Stella's childhood, wore a fez to work, but under pressure from Felicie and the other children, who felt it made him seem too *a la turka* (too Turkish, and thereby too old-fashioned), eventually, though not without a protest, gave it up.

Stella's two grandmothers were cocooned in layers and layers of mysterious clothes, undergarments covered by blouses, skirts, belts, and robes, with that unfathomable hair of theirs always concealed under a toque. Stella never saw either grandmother undressed; she never saw them with their hair exposed, let alone down; she never even saw them at the Turkish bath wearing a striped *peshtamel.* Their bodies were a mystery.

Much about the body remained a mystery, for the longest time.

22

One of Stella's earliest memories:

She is two and a half, maybe three years old. Her mother instructs her to walk down the block to Ermana Dalva's house and ask her, as Stella hears it, to give her some *teneme aki*. Stella does as she's told. Ermana Dalva invites her to sit down. Stella waits patiently. After half an hour she says to Ermana Dalva, "Are you going to give me some *teneme aki?*" "Yes, I am. Just be patient." She waits another half an hour and asks again. Ermana Dalva tells her to be a little more patient. She gives her a biscuit to eat. Is the biscuit *teneme aki?* Stella doesn't think so. After another half an hour, Ermana Dalva tells her she can go home.

"But what about the *teneme aki?*"

"I've already given it to you."

Teneme aki, in Judeo-Spanish: "keep me here" but, implicitly, "watch over me" or "look after me." Sometimes it was said in Turkish: *otur burda* (stay here). No one in the Juderia had nannies or babysitters; when a mother needed to run an errand, or have a moment to herself, a moment of peace, she would send her child to a friend nearby and tell the child to ask for some *teneme aki* or, perhaps, a bit of *otur burda*.

This was Stella's first brush with the confusion, the mystery, the power and complexity of language, and it would stay with her, in one way or another, all the rest of her life. How could it be otherwise, growing up where she did, in an ever-shifting Tower of Babel of communication?

I ask her to help me understand who spoke what and in which context.

Judeo-Spanish was the language of the Juderia, spoken in every home. Stella's grandmothers, in addition, understood liturgical Hebrew. Her maternal grandmother, Sara Notrica, also spoke Turkish and some Greek. Both women lived under the Italians for nearly twenty years but never learned to speak a single word of that language.

Stella's father wrote Judeo-Spanish using Solitreo, a Sephardic form of Hebrew script that allowed the writer to transcribe the language into Hebrew letters by spelling words phonetically (from *soletrar*, to spell, in Portuguese).

In the next generation, only Morris learned Solitreo, before he left for California in 1920, and, in any event, in the early twentieth century Judeo-Spanish speakers had already begun to write the language in Roman letters, also spelling most words phonetically and with a bedeviling combination of imaginativeness and inconsistency.

Yehuda learned to read and write Hebrew at school. Miriam learned Hebrew by ear; she knew prayers, songs, and the occasional words or phrases. She spoke some Turkish and some Greek; Yehuda spoke Turkish, because for much of his life he did business in that language.

Both he and Miriam understood more Italian than their mothers but far less than their children.

As with other families in the Juderia the Levi children attended school in a language their parents neither read nor wrote—actually two *different* languages.

The older siblings attended the Alliance Israélite Universelle, which advanced its mission in Rhodes, as it did all through the Middle East, of giving children a Western-style education that was at once religious and modern and was intended to release them from the "prison" (as it was rather condescendingly described) of the language they spoke at home. But just as the Alliance was solidifying its linguistic and cultural hold on the island, colonizing the minds of young girls like Selma, Sara, and Felicie, who read French romances and went around the Juderia greeting their classmates and friends with a fluty *bonjour* and *bonsoir* and (for Rosh Hashana) *bonnes fêtes*, along came the Italians.

In 1925, two years after Stella was born and while Italy was solidifying administrative control of Rhodes, the Alliance metamorphosed into the Scuole Ebraiche Italiane (plural because there was one for the boys, one for the girls). Out went the French teachers, the French manners, the French textbooks (and romances), and in came everything Italian:

language, music, literature, history, soccer, and (some) food. The three younger Levi children—Victor, Renée, and Stella herself—came of age in a linguistically and culturally distinct world from their parents and older siblings. Not quite overnight, though sometimes it felt like that, all the younger people now began going around greeting *their* friends with *buongiorno* and *buonasera*.

Virtually no one in Rhodes spoke English, only a family named Cohen, who lived outside of the Juderia and whose father gave private lessons, and a tour guide called Cordobal, who made a living by accompanying the few English-speaking tourists who came to the island.

23

The different nicknames and honorifics used in the Juderia comprise an interesting footnote to the many languages spoken there. As in certain other Spanish-speaking settings, men and women of Stella's grandparents' and parents' generations were typically referred to as *Ermano* and *Ermana*. ("It was not unlike African American people here referring to each other as Brother and Sister.") Not every woman was *Ermana*, however. Sometimes, possibly because she had come from elsewhere, or had lived abroad, or for reasons Stella has not been able to work out, she would instead be *Madame*—as in *Madame Leon* or, in some contexts, *Madame Miriam*, for Stella's mother. And in more formal contexts she might also be identified as being connected to her husband: *Ermana Sara Notrica de Moshe* was Stella's grandmother, Moshe's wife, and Miriam was *Ermana Miriam de Yehuda Levi*—basically Yehuda's Miriam.

These appellations became more complicated if you were the firstborn of a family, in which case you would be referred to as, for example, *Ermana Behora Soriano* or *Ermana Behora Franco*—both of whom were Miriam's friends—since *Behora* (for women) and *Behor* (for men) meant firstborn and was often mentioned.

A different way still of showing respect was *Señor* or *Señora*: *Señora*

Miriam de Moshe Levi, or just *Señora Miriam Levi. Señora* was a particularly meaningful word in the community. Before the Italians came (that is: before *Señora* became confused with *Signora*), it was also a given name—in fact it was Stella's older sister Selma's given name: she was born Señora Levi, named for her great-grandmother Señora Halfon.

As a given name, Señora is believed to pay homage to Doña Gracia Mendes Nasi (*Doña* being a variant of *Señora*), who was born in Portugal in or around 1510 to a family of conversos and had a life worthy of a picaresque novel: she was a businesswoman, a banker, the backer of printing presses, a smuggler of other conversos out of Spain and Portugal, an endower of yeshivas and synagogues, and late in life a proto-Zionist who managed to convince Suleiman the Magnificent to grant her a long-term lease of land near Tiberias in the Galilee, where she helped to revive threadbare towns as places to resettle immigrant Jews.

"If you were lucky to be called Señora," Stella tells me, "you bore your name with great pride."

Judeo-Spanish, Hebrew, Turkish, Greek, French, Italian . . . names, nicknames, namesakes: after Stella lays all this out for me, I find myself wanting to know which is "her" language, the one she thinks in, the one in which she expresses herself most deeply. I hesitate to call it her mother tongue, since that would have to be Judeo-Spanish. Her native tongue, then? Her dominant tongue? Is it even right to think that there is just one?

However you categorize it, Stella doesn't hesitate to answer that this language is Italian: "From the very beginning I adored the Italian language. It sounded beautiful to my ear, it resembled my language, and it felt like a language I was born into. It was also the language I was educated in and that opened up my world when I was still in Rhodes."

Opened up in what ways, I ask her.

"My mind. My friendships." Her eyes shimmer. "My more-than-friendships."

"So those boyfriends were Italian, were they?"

"That part comes later, Michael—*forse.*"

• • •

46

I try to make sense of what it means to belong linguistically and in many ways culturally to a country that you didn't grow up in and didn't visit for the first time until you were in your early twenties, and under such unusual circumstances, as a survivor of a concentration camp.

Does Stella consider herself Italian? What does that even mean in her case?

She thinks for a moment then says, "Now that is a different question. No, I don't consider myself Italian. Even though I lived in Italy for two years, my point of origin is not Italian. It's the Jewish community of the island of Rhodes, which originated half a millennium earlier in Spain and, for a time, a brief time, fell under Italian control."

She pauses. "A mouthful, I know. But there is no short answer, not one that I've come up with, anyway."

Stella's father, she adds, never once identified as Turkish *or* Italian. It was not how people of his generation thought. His entire experience of life was filtered through his Judaism, and he passed this connection down to his children. Even though Stella grew up to be a nonbeliever, she says that, in Rhodes, if she identified with anything, it was her Judaism, which organized the weeks, the seasons, the holidays—their whole lives, their whole world.

"This is my heritage," Stella says. "But my identity is something altogether different. It's fluid. I think of myself as neither one thing or another. I've been that way since childhood, and I've felt it more and more strongly as I've advanced through my life."

Several years after Stella and I have this conversation, she and I attend an evening during which the historians Saul Friedländer and Carlo Ginzburg discuss Friedländer's new memoir, and the next time we meet I ask her about some of his remarks.

I was particularly struck, I tell her, by one of the first things that Friedländer said: "If language is where one lives, then I have no home, because I have no fixed language."

Stella nods. "Yes, I think that's true of many of us who became severed from our points of origin."

Friedländer went on to explain, as I paraphrase him to Stella, that he once wrote in French and now writes in English but has not found "permanency" in either language. He doesn't live in his name, because he changed it five times. It took him years, he said, to know who he was. He wrote about the Holocaust but didn't find his own voice until he wrote his own history. He had to land in a place, he said, that is no place. Eventually he found that identity in memory.

"Without my memory, I'm not sure I'd have any idea of who I am," Stella says. "But even here my identity remains connected to language. Judeo-Spanish actually *helps* me remember. I hear a song, a phrase, a word—and it instantly takes me back into the Juderia of my youth."

"Which is nevertheless still not your home."

"*Nous serons toujours exilés*," she says, appropriating (and slightly modifying) a line from Racine's *Esther*.

Her home is not a place, Stella continues, because Rhodes, the Rhodes of today, is not her place, and cannot be. She has no real home; like many Jews, and most survivors, she will always be an exile. She went to Los Angeles, to her family, what was left of her family, but did not feel at home there. She went to Israel but did not feel at home there either. She is most at home in New York, she says, because New York is itself made up of so many exiles, so many wanderers like her.

Ginzburg, I remind her, asked Friedländer if the experience of exile gave him a chance to be something more in life, to grow.

"In my case it has," she says, "though exile, trust me, comes at a price."

24

The *scuola femminile,* a Catholic school outside of the Juderia, thirty minutes away on foot, past the mosque, past the bridge; as Felicie had before her, Stella began to study there at the age of twelve, with the *suore* (the *suore d'Ivrea* was their order), enrolling in the rigorous *quarta ginnasio.* (In the Italian system, *quarta* and *quinta ginnasio* come between middle school and high school and are followed by the *prima, seconda,* and *terza liceo,* three years of high school instruction that culminate in an exam called the *maturità* that, if passed, allows a student to proceed to university.)

Every year a handful of girls in the Juderia—in Stella's year they numbered just five—gathered in the morning to set off for the long walk across town. In winter, they wore black skirts, cream-colored shirts, and black socks; in spring, as soon as the weather changed, they traded the black socks for white. Every strand of their hair was in place, their notebooks crisp and immaculate, their *grembiulini* freshly ironed.

When Stella walked through the doors to the school for the first time, "*Tutto ad un tratto,* vroom"—all of a sudden, *boom*—a new world was opened to her, subjects, possibilities that she had only dreamed of before. She'd felt primed for what lay ahead by Felicie, by stories her grandmother had told her and that she'd read in the Bible and in other books, but this was the real thing. Literature. Latin. Ancient Greek. History. With teachers to teach her, guide her, help her. She was excited and also, yes, fearful. She was afraid of making a *brutta figura,* she was afraid she might not be smart enough, she was afraid of being tested and testing herself, but her thirst was so great to know as much as she could as quickly as she could that she largely overcame her fears.

At the *scuola femminile* Stella mastered Latin and arithmetic and deepened her understanding of French grammar, and from Sister Teresa, who was young and vibrant, she learned batches of Italian poetry by heart, like Leopardi's "A Silvia," which seventy-five years later and half a world away she recites for me in an old-school, theatrical voice, her chin up and posture erect, just the way it must have been when in front of the class she was asked to stand and declaim—

> *Silvia, rimembri ancora*
> *Quel tempo della tua vita mortale,*
> *Quando beltà splendea*
> *Negli occhi tuoi ridenti e fuggitivi . . .*

At school Stella competed for the gold medal for best in the class, fiercely, with Silvia Rozio, whose father was a broom-maker and whose older brothers were among the smartest boys in the neighborhood. Silvia won the gold; Stella took the silver: *Vediamo un pò se sarai brava come Felicie.*

"Apparently I wasn't *brava* enough," Stella says.

On Wednesdays, while the other girls studied religion, Rabbi Albagli, with his tiny eyeglasses, came to teach them about Judaism while a sister kept watch, not merely because he was the only man among girls but because she wanted to make sure they paid attention. They were there to learn, even about their own religion, no matter what.

Stella says they were never made to feel uncomfortable because of their Judaism, not overtly, but of course they had the rabbi on Wednesday and they never went to mass; instead they waited in the garden, doing their homework or playing, so they were marked as different, excluded. During May, the month of the Madonna, there were many events they were released from, but on the plus side she learned a lot about Catholicism from her schoolmates that she never would have otherwise.

"I was one step closer to my dream," Stella tells me, her eyes shining. One step closer to taking that suitcase and setting off for university in Italy.

Almost as a footnote Stella drops in one more detail to her description of school.

After the war, she tells me, she went to try to find Sister Teresa in Rome, in Trastevere, where she heard that she and some of the other *suore* were then living; she had a question to ask her, a question she would have liked to ask all of them, if she could. Twice she went to look for them and twice she failed.

What was the question?

"Oh, it was very simple," Stella says evenly. "I wanted to know, having been our teachers and the teachers of my sister and her friends, so many of us, where they happened to be on the day we were rounded up.

I wanted to ask them why they never came to make inquiries or to object, why afterward, on the day we left, they never even came to say so much as good-bye."

25

The five girls from the Juderia weren't the only Jewish girls to study with the *suore*. They were joined by the daughters of certain of those well-to-do families who had moved out of the neighborhood and lived differently from everyone else.

In what way did they live differently? Was it simply a matter of their having better houses?

Better houses, bigger ones, yes, but not just that. It was as if they'd crossed over into another world, another century. They lived with appliances, and proper bathrooms, and a staff. Even though they lived far closer to school than the girls in the Juderia, some of them only a few blocks away, they came with a driver, who would open the door for them, and out they would step, first one foot in one perfectly polished shoe, then the other. Among these families were the Menasces, cousins of Stella's mother on the Notrica side, part of the banking branch of the family. One afternoon Evelina Menasce invited Stella to lunch at her house with their classmate Bella Almeleh, another girl from the Juderia who, when she sat down at the table, widened her eyes and leaned in to whisper to Stella while pointing discretely, "*Dio*, there's a knife!"

The Menasces had seen how people of a certain class lived in Paris and Rome and Athens: their whole manner of living was modernized, urban; urbane. In modern European homes the tables were set with knives, whereas in the Juderia they ate with only a fork; a fork and a piece of bread, since most of their dishes were made, in the Turkish fashion, of small components, everything already chopped or diced or sliced, and at any rate softened by fire and time. Who needed a knife on the table, one more implement to wash, dry, and put away? They were large families, there were already so many plates, so much cutlery . . . and the bread, well, it soaked up the sauce, it tasted so good . . .

"It's not as if we were exactly *primitive*," Stella adds. "It just wasn't how it was done in the Juderia, when I was a girl, to set the table with knives."

It was as if they'd crossed over into another world. I ask Stella what that means, exactly. Surely it wasn't simply because they set their tables with knives, and had those appliances, and bathrooms with showers and tubs?

"In a way," she answers, "it was."

Not merely plumbing but water, water in general, Stella explains, is a story, a dozen stories—a capsule portrait of the Juderia unto itself.

A well stood at the center of their *kortijo* when Stella was growing up. It was true, yes, that the Italians brought running water into the Juderia (though indoor showers and baths were still a rarity) and sewage pipes for plumbing, but that didn't mean the well ran dry—the opposite. Until the very end the Levis still drew water from the well to wash the floors and the windows, and since even after the arrival of the Italians there were still no refrigerators, they used it as a cooler, lowering bottles in a large basket to keep them fresh and, in summer, storing watermelons, also in a basket, belowground, which as a consequence stayed extra sweet and crisp. The upstairs neighbor who had no well of her own wanted to share theirs—she even went so far one day as to mount a pulley from her terrace and dangle a rope down into the courtyard—but Selma was adamantly against it, as she didn't want the mess that had to be mopped away afterward. "The screaming over that, you cannot imagine."

Then there was *la dulse*—"And I have no idea why it was called that . . . *dulse* . . . *dulce* . . . *dolce* . . . sweet? When in fact it means the opposite?" Every now and then the shamash from the synagogue, alerted by the rabbi, hurried through the streets urgently crying, "*La dulse, la dulse!*" And Miriam and the other women raced to fill up bottles and bowls and pots, and to cover the cleaning water with a towel, because they knew that, for a certain amount of time, not long, a few hours perhaps, possibly as long as half a day (it was never precisely stated beforehand), the water that came from the taps would be poisonous, on account of an evil spirit passing through the Juderia. No one should drink or wash during this time, and no one did.

Victor did once run to the Mandrakio, the promenade along the sea, to have a glass of water in one of the bars just to show how absurd this tradition was, upsetting Miriam, who was a believer, still, in such things. And Felicie, well, it's easy to know what she thought: she had nothing to do with *la dulce*, naturally.

Stella has never gotten to the bottom of *la dulce*, and nor did her cousin in her book, or anyone else we can find. She wonders if the custom goes back to the Ottoman period, when people didn't have any running water at all, and those who didn't have wells obtained their water from communal fountains—two were near the synagogues and two or three were elsewhere in the Juderia and one was in the Turkeria nearby. Maybe, at certain times, and for certain reasons, the water went bad? Maybe, when there was conflict, someone in fact contaminated it?

Possibly it had something to do with another custom concerning water, which was to empty every receptacle as soon as someone in the house had died. I find two possible explanations: one is a belief that the angel of death cleansed his death sword in standing water, if he could find it; the other is that *any* evil spirit could take refuge in the water and harm the living. I ask Stella if she's ever heard of either, and she shakes her head. "So many of these things just *happened*, you know. No one told us why."

26

One of the sacrosanct rituals of the week was a visit to the hammam, where Miriam and the girls went each Thursday, occasionally on Friday, for a minimum of two hours, often longer. Miriam was a favorite of an attendant named Fatmà. Even when the Turkish bath was crowded, Fatmà always welcomed "Miriam Hanum" (Madame Miriam) and managed to reserve the largest room for the Levi women to change from their street clothes to a *peshtamel* (a Turkish towel of absorbent cotton, usually striped) and elevated wooden clogs called *takos* in Judeo-Spanish or *zoccoli* in Italian, and set them up with a *stregadura* (in the Judeo-Spanish of Rhodes, a rough mitt for scrubbing away the dead skin) and a *yashmak* (Turkish again: a head scarf, sometimes with sequins, to wrap around their damp hair when they finished). It's not surprising that Stella mixes together the different languages as she describes the lay of the land at the hammam, where Turkish and Jewish and occasionally some Italian (but no Greek) women spent the afternoon in peaceful camaraderie.

The visit began in the sauna—scalding—and proceeded to a marble-clad room where basins were fitted with hot and cold spigots that filled a *taz*, a beaten metal bowl, typically of copper, which they used, or Fatmà used, to scrub their bodies in conjunction with the coarse mitt that took off a layer of skin. Afterward, she would draw a fine white comb through their hair. "It felt like a part of yourself, not just your body, was being scoured away, so that you could be refreshed, more than that, almost reborn, every week. I don't think I've been so clean ever since in my life."

The basins weren't for immersing oneself in—though such a basin did exist, in a separate part of the hammam, and was used exclusively by Jewish women as their mikvah, since there was no longer a mikvah in the Juderia in Stella's day. (Two were discovered years later, both attached to synagogues.)

Before they left, Fatmà served them coffee, or lemonade, and sweets, and daubed them with *agua de flor* whose main ingredient was jasmine.

"Would you like a whiff?" Stella asks me.

"Of *agua de flor*? Is there a new hammam in Greenwich Village that I don't know about?"

She laughs, then slips into the kitchen, returning with a tiny glass vial whose contents are nearly evaporated. "I brought it back with me from Turkey years ago," she says, then she uncorks it and hands it over.

Jasmine, yes. Pronounced. Maybe also a touch of orange blossom.

"Do you cook with it?" I ask. "Is that why you keep it in the kitchen?"

She shakes her head. "Once upon a time women used it when they felt faint, and so it was a handy thing to have on hand."

Women, I point out, don't often seem to feel faint these days, or actually *to* faint.

"Equality forces you to give up certain things," Stella says with a smile.

27

The Turkish bath was also the setting for one of Stella's favorite events when she was small: the *banyo de novya*, where the soon-to-be bride attended the mikvah and participated in the henna-painting party afterward that included dancing, singing the *kantigas de novya*, and tasting the mountains of sweets that had been prepared by the bride's mother and aunts for days beforehand.

As a girl, Stella loved watching the rituals of the wedding play out in the Juderia too. A week or two before the actual day, the bride's *ashugar*, that trousseau that included all those linens she'd spent years embroidering, was delivered to her future husband's house as a little band of Greek musicians assembled with their mandolin and tambourines to accompany the splendor, which was balanced on large trays and carried on the heads of people hired to transport the linens, yes, but also often glassware and dishes and housewares and the silver bestowed, in some families, by the grandmother. Then, on the day itself, the father or older brother of the bride delivered the young woman to her husband in the synagogue, and afterward everyone would walk in a procession to the bride's family's house or a friend's, if it was larger or had a garden, or a hotel, the Regina or the Albergo delle Rose, if the woman came from one of the better-off families, for the party that followed.

At the beginning of the war, Stella's teacher, and (later) friend, Luigi Noferini attended one of these weddings, where the young people put on records. It was the first time Stella had seen him dance, the first time she had danced with a man outside of her group of friends, ever. By then, though, weddings had become more of a rarity as more and more young people, mainly men, had left the island.

•　　•　　•

This talk about weddings leads us back to Felicie. Did she ever show any interest in boys? Did no one ever captivate her?

"We didn't talk about things like that," Stella tells me. "She sat with Robert Cohen, I've told you, sometimes across the room, sometimes on the *canapé* together, talking deep into the night. But it never seemed to be more than talk, at least not to me. And besides he could never get his socks to match."

I ask Stella if her parents were ever worried about Felicie, the oldest sister still at home, unmarried, with no prospects, no apparent plan for her future. And her answer, as ever with Felicie, is that if it were any girl *other* than Felicie, they would have been. Most of the parents in the Juderia behaved as if they were living back in time by fifty, a hundred years. A woman who didn't get married had something wrong with her and set off a tornado of concern, but not Felicie: she was firm; she wouldn't have anything to do with marriage; she was a free thinker. "Maybe something happened to her," Stella speculates. "I mean physically. Intimately. If it did, I never knew . . ."

She withdraws into a moment of silence. "Sometimes I wonder if Felicie thought of herself as unattractive. She wasn't, but it occurs to me now that whenever we left the Turkish baths with our hair in a *yashmak*, Felicie alone would draw the scarf across her face, the way the Turkish women did. And not just then. She took every opportunity to turn away, cover her face, avoid being photographed, avoid being seen, period, in *that* way . . . in many ways."

After another silence, I ask, carefully, if perhaps Felicie didn't care for boys.

"I don't think that was it," Stella says. "But I don't know that either. We *certainly* never discussed such matters. You have to remember she always treated me, regarded me, as a little girl, the little sister, which in essence I was."

I ask Stella if there were any people in the community she knew to be gay, and how they were seen or treated if so. And if it was ever discussed, even in private. She tells me that she didn't even have a *concept* of homosexuality until after the war, when she came to America and understood many more things about human nature. In America, she realized retrospectively, she and Felicie read and loved writers who happened to be gay, like Verlaine and Rimbaud and Proust, and she was able to look back at one of her dearest friends, a boy who was very handsome, blond, and attentive to his mother. He used to hang out with the girls; he had a gentle soul. Only in hindsight did she see that he was likely gay. He too died in the camps.

"In another time or place," Stella says ruminatively, "think what his life would have been."

His life, like other lives in the Juderia?

"But he was doubly harmed. He could not be himself . . . and then he could not *be*."

28

There was a hammam for the men—more opulent than the one for the women—but Yehuda didn't go there very often. He preferred to bathe at home.

As there was no bathtub or shower at the Levi house or, with one or maybe two exceptions, in any other house in the Juderia, Miriam had rigged a system in the *kortijo*: an enormous pot for boiling water, another for cold water, and a curtain to create a tiny cubicle inside of which Yehuda took his weekly wash, with Miriam combining hot and cold from separate pots and pouring it over his head, as needed—a homespun shower.

This, like the visits to the hammam, happened only once a week, in preparation for the sabbath, though if a need came up, of course, they washed during the week, and always their hands and faces. And in the summer they had the sea, where showers had been installed by those modernizing Italians; cold showers, but showers nevertheless.

As for going to the bathroom: this took place in the courtyard as well, in a tiny closet with a window fitted into its door, where instead of toilet paper a terra cotta vessel was kept full of clean water and each member of the family had her, or his, own sponge to facilitate washing up afterward.

"*Purim Purim lanu,*" went an old expression in the Juderia, "*Pesah en la mano*"—Purim is here, Passover is near (or, less mellifluously, *at hand*). And Passover meant cleaning, and washing, everything in sight. Everything out of sight too.

As soon as the sometimes raucous festivities of Purim wound down, Stella tells me, you could feel a shift in the energy of the neighborhood as mothers, daughters, and Greek or sometimes Jewish maids hired just for these weeks would begin the most rigorous housekeeping of the year. They emptied out closets, cupboards, and drawers; they moved every last table and chair; Persian and Turkish rugs were pulled up, scrubbed with a mixture of water and vinegar, and hung out to dry on the terrace. The chandeliers were washed, the silver polished, the special set of china brought out of the cupboard where it sat untouched all year long. Houses were whitewashed outside and in. Then came a final Juderia-wide assault on dirt and dust and grime as you even washed the patch of street in front of your door. In fact neighbors made careful arrangements among themselves to ensure the dirty water from one house would not spill over to the next: Ermana Leon was starting on Thursday morning, so Ermana Levi planned to start a few hours later. The next-door neighbor would follow an hour after that, and so on down the block until they came to the end of the street, the end of the dirt, the end of the day.

Stella shakes her head. "It's a way of living that you don't understand, you can't understand," she says. "Even my siblings and I, when we got together later in life, we couldn't understand. All that time and energy, hours, days, sometimes weeks—simply to clean?"

The days before Passover weren't *only* about housework. A particular form of anxiety thrummed through the neighborhood as the holiday approached, especially during Stella's early childhood. "Take the longer route," Miriam occasionally warned the children as they were leaving the walled city. "Don't go by the Greeks." Sometimes they listened to her, sometimes they didn't; but during Passover for sure they did, because on Passover they were concerned that Greeks, some Greeks, might throw stones at them. The classic explanation connected the stone-throwing to a revival of blood libel, the belief that the Jews used Christian blood in the preparation of their matzahs, and in fact there had been a distressing local case where the Greeks accused the Jews of a ritual murder of a Christian boy, which led to blockades, false imprisonment, torture, and trials before the community was exonerated—but this had happened in 1840. More likely, old, settled tensions were rekindled by the alacrity with which the Jews had embraced those modernizing Italians, and at any rate the stone-throwing seems to have petered out by the time Stella was a teenager.

Yom Kippur was another holiday that came with a water ritual. As this holiest day of the year drew to a close, a Turkish man rode into the Juderia on his donkey, bringing large vessels, the ones typical of Rhodes that looked like amphorae and inevitably evoked the amphorae of the ancient world; they were filled with water from nearby Rodino, which was considered the sweetest, most delicious water on the island. The gentleman waited patiently outside the synagogue for the services to end, when everyone rushed outside and availed themselves of the pure water of Rodino, thereby ending the fast.

Leaping ahead now in time: The grandmothers die, taking so many of the old ways with them. The Italians settle in and bring so many of the new ways with *them*, including this: Yehuda, who didn't even like to go as far as the Turkish baths, began to follow his doctor's counsel and, to treat his diabetes, rode a bus to Kallithea to take . . . the waters, of course, whose diuretic and other properties had been discovered, or rediscovered, by the Italians, who put up a fanciful Ottoman bathhouse with exaggerated Moorish arches and domes that would be heavily bombed during the war.

Water drew Miriam, who never traveled anywhere on her own, not ever, even farther afield. Several times, for several days at a time, she packed a bag and took a boat to the nearby island of Nisyros: more water cures still. However modern it may have seemed for a woman like Stella's mother to make this excursion, the waters themselves went back in time, as they had been first identified by no one less than Hippocrates himself.

29

In the Juderia everyone knew everyone's business. More than that: everyone was *in* everyone's business. And that was in part because in the Juderia they were all related to each other—except when they chose not to be.

I'm confused. "Literally related?"

"In a way . . ."

I ask Stella for a reality check. Might she calculate, roughly, how many people she was *actually* related to in the community?

She begins with her first cousins and counts: eight, nine . . . twelve. Second cousins, well, if you include the Halfons, the Menasces (or Menascés—the spelling changes depending on the branch of the family), the Notricas, the Pihases . . . forty-five, fifty maybe. ("My grandparents were cousins, don't forget, which cuts down some on the numbers.") Second cousins once removed? Third? She didn't even know all of them, even half of them; she was closer, she says, to certain friends and classmates, but if I insist on a figure, all right then: 150, 160. Likely more.

That's 160, 170 people in all, or 10 percent of the entire population of the Juderia, if you do the math using the numbers from 1944.

Related to 10 percent of the people you live among? Is such a thing possible?

"Not only is it possible. I'm still meeting people today that I didn't know I was related to."

Just the other afternoon, she tells me, she received a call from a woman in New Jersey who had been born in Rhodesia. Her mother was in Auschwitz with Stella and survived, and her aunt Flora—the last in a large family—was in Stella's class at school, but died in the camps. Rosa Israel was her mother, and her grandmother, Ermana Sarotta, it turned out, was a Menasce married to a Pihas, who was a cousin of Stella's Notrica grandmother because *her* mother was a Pihas, and the father, of course ("of course"!), was Mazliah Notrica, the progenitor of the family of bankers . . .

I write down what Stella tells me, but do not really follow. Or rather I follow the gist: they were all connected—interconnected.

—except when they chose not be:

Even the very structure of the Juderia bound them all together. The Levis' terrace was separated by a low parapet, scarcely a foot high, from the terrace of the Turiel family, which meant that Stella peeked when her neighbors Boaz and Elliot Turiel were born, at home of course, with the help of *la komadre*, or midwife (a lifetime later, Stella and Elliot are still friends). She didn't even have to go downstairs to learn the news.

Like the terraces, the *kortijos* opened up one family, one life, to another. All day long women called across these courtyards to ask what was being prepared for dinner, why this daughter or that son had gone out with this son or that daughter, who (like Sara, *la kayijera*) had been out late the night before, who was unwell, who had had a nightmare or a pleasant dream. And then there was all that singing, not just within a single home but as a way of connecting home to home, family to family. When Tia Rosa visited she sang to the children to put an end to squabbling or to lift everyone's spirits, and the sound of her voice would be heard through one of the open windows or across a *kortijo*. The next thing Stella knew, a neighbor would lean out of *her* window and call out, "*Ah, kantando estash*," and soon an impromptu chorus of women popped their heads out of windows and doorways to sing,

Una pastora yo ami
Una ija ermoza
De mi chikez yo la adori
Mas ke eya no ami
De mi chikez yo la adori
Mas ke eya no ami

Eighty, ninety years after she first heard it, in an ever-fainter voice, Stella sings me this song about a boy's love for a shepherdess, a beautiful girl he loved from his childhood, when he loved no one else, and not for the first time I feel I can see back beyond even Stella's youth to her mother's and her mother's before her, and maybe even farther back than that.

"Incredible," I say. And Stella says, nodding, "Incredible—but also, depending on where you were in your life, potentially claustrophobic."

When Stella was a girl, she says, it all seemed so friendly—"cozy," we would say in English—but then as she grew older, it all began to feel *too* cozy. The women in the neighborhood would look out the window when she left in the evening and again when she returned; they would take note of what she was wearing and even in what direction she was heading. "And then when I was older and began to spend time with young men, Italian men . . . oh, how the tongues wagged."

Not Miriam's though: she was against such things. She was uninterested in hearing gossip about her children or anyone else's.

She said to Stella: *Your voice is too high, the neighbors will hear.* Or: *Slip out more quietly, why don't you?* Or: *Secrets, we keep at home.*

Stella did her best, but the eyes were sharp, the ears were like a dog's. They picked up on even the faintest of signals.

30

Everyone knew about everyone's disagreements too. And where, and to whom, these people went to try to resolve them. Stella's grandmother Sara Notrica was one such person—a healer in a different sense. A couple in crisis, the husband, say, wanting another child, the wife, after giving birth to six children, finished, bone-tired, worried about the scarcity of food, of clothes, of money: How did they resolve such conundrums? They went to the old woman, and she would make a suggestion, impart advice.

What suggestion, which advice?

"No one left the door open during these conversations."

Stella knew they went. She knew they closed the door. She didn't know what they said *exactly*.

Still . . . did she know if, for instance, the issue was about more children, whether the couple practiced birth control? "They had their way, though it didn't always work out."

And . . . and when the birth control didn't work? Were any of these pregnancies ended?

A close friend of Stella's—"I will never tell you her name"—became pregnant. She tried to go to the Turkish baths; occasionally something managed to happen there. A different young woman, older than Stella, knew what to do because her boyfriend had shared the information; her parents arranged for her to travel to Italy by plane. It was a great rarity, to travel by plane to Italy. In the case of this young woman only her parents knew, and Stella, and one other friend.

Was it scandalous?

"Naturally."

What did they say?

"The story went around that there was a place. They always referred to it as *terme*—baths—for a cure. A physical cure, a mental cure. You know."

"No one wondered why she didn't simply stay home and have an *enserradura*?"

"Pregnancy was one thing the *enserradura* didn't take care of. And besides, this was in the early forties. We were living in a more modern world by then."

31

In a book about Rhodes I come across an insight offered by its author, Nathan Shachar, that I bring to Stella the next time we meet: "Only a minority of persons have the presence of mind and verbal gifts to observe and digest all that takes place as one life form begins to give way to another."

He seems, uncannily, to be describing Stella. As a girl in Rhodes she certainly observed; she was certainly attuned to the changing life forms around her; then and since she has certainly digested everything she saw. What made her that sort of person, though, one of that minority who had, or developed, that presence of mind, and those perceptual and verbal skills?

"I don't know if it's a question I can answer," Stella says. "It's a bit like asking, 'Why do you have brown hair, or green eyes?'"

She reflects for a moment. "But I think . . . I think if I was able to see the changes that were going on around me, it may have been because I first had an awareness, an understanding that there was a world *beyond*. I had a deep curiosity about what was out there, and I think that's what made me sensitive to difference. I lived in the Juderia, but I knew that, just a few blocks away, there was more than the Juderia. I paid attention to people who seemed different, like my uncle Isaac Amato who, though he worked as a tinsmith, was in fact a cultivated man, entirely self-taught, a serious reader. I grew up on an island, but I knew that it was just a speck of land in a vast sea. It was something I felt in my body, my very self . . ."

Stella remembers, as a girl, looking out on the horizon and knowing that across all the blue lay worlds, other worlds, other ways. She knew this because of the stories she first read; because of the history of Rhodes with all of its invasions and transformations that she studied at school and learned about from Felicie; because of the boats she saw docking at the port, some delivering the first tourists to the island and others the first immigrants, who were pausing on their way to Palestine; and because of the signs of elsewhere that were imprinted on her family—on their past, their work, even their names and nicknames.

Her father dealt in wood and coal that he imported and supplied locally. Imported from where? Romania maybe, or the Ukraine; but in any event, like many goods, they likely passed through Turkey. Stella cannot say for sure, and when Stella cannot say something for sure, or close to sure, she prefers not to. The point, though, is that these items came from abroad, as did the spices that her great-grandfather Notrica had dealt in a generation earlier. Already right there, in her family, was an understanding, in the most basic way, of a wider world that supplied products to Rhodes from far-off places, typically via the age-old crossroads at nearby İzmir.

Then, of course, there was her grandmother Sara, with her regular trips to the Holy Land, though it turns out she wasn't the only member of the family who traveled there. Stella's great-uncle on her grandfather Notrica's side, Yehuda Notrica, the youngest of her grandfather's siblings and the only one who was alive in Stella's time, was affectionately referred to as Haji Yehuda because of all the hajis he made—not to Mecca, but to Jerusalem.

A man given a nickname that alluded to his propensity for travel: that made an impression. It made her wonder, as did the fact that the vibrant, vivid personalities of her older sisters were now reduced to communication via post, another powerful sign of elsewhere that became almost visceral whenever the mailman came flying into the Juderia on his bicycle, sounding his bell as he approached: who was lucky, this day, to receive updates from France, or Turkey, or America? The news that a letter had come sped through the neighborhood, of course. Information was shared; elsewhere came, briefly, into the house. Elsewhere became here.

32

Elsewhere was imprinted, as well, on the very buildings of Rhodes: on the Greek ruins on Monte Smith and on the enduring muscular *palazzi* put up by the Knights, traces of whose hegemony over the island extended even to the Juderia, where on a building not far from the house where Stella grew up there hung (and hangs still) one of their coats of arms.

A particularly substantial building belonging to the Knights anchored the Kay Ancha, one of the main *piazze* of the Juderia; after the Italians came, they installed a cultural institute within its noble stone walls, the Dante Alighieri Society, which extended the notion of beyond in several important ways. The Dante Alighieri housed an extensive library, and naturally nothing took a young, curious, and alert boy or girl so far beyond as books. Among the youth of the Juderia who made the most use of the library first were—unsurprisingly—Felicie and Robert Cohen, along with a young man named Giuseppe Hazan, whom Stella affectionately called Yosefacci and used to tease about his intellectual aspirations when he went off for long walks during which he talked about philosophy with his teacher, Frate Angelino: "*Ma, Yosefacci, vai a fare il peripatetico?*" (There's gentle mockery, or perhaps envy, in the way she asked him if he was going to walk and talk philosophy on the model of the Aristotelian Peripatetic school.) The Dante Alighieri offered lectures too, and was a locale of such importance in the neighborhood that in May 1929, when the king of Italy, Victor Emmanuel III, visited the Juderia, Turkish carpets were laid down, covering the whole of the piazza up to and including the stairs to the Dante Alighieri, where the king was blessed by the grand rabbi Reuben Eliyahu Israel himself.

Stella too frequented the library, but almost as important, the Dante Alighieri provided a connection to the wider world when, each summer, a new batch of Italian university students assembled there for monthlong courses. Stella used to see them arrive and wonder about these bright, ebullient young kids: where they had come from, where they were going, whether she might find her place among them one day.

"I often reflect on that building," Stella says, "with its suggestive coat of arms and handsome staircase that were there in the time of my great-grandparents, my great-great-grandparents—all the way back. These people, going about their lives in the Juderia: What did they think when they looked up and saw this coat of arms that connected the neighborhood to its long-ago rulers? Did it make them speculate, as I did, about the people who had come before, and had left, and how everything changed over the centuries? How the people disappeared, but their buildings endured?"

A silence opens up between us. I sense Stella weighing whether to share a thought, a detail. This time she first says outright that she's not even sure she should add this one thing because it seems so odd, maybe so inappropriate. Then:

"I don't know how you'll hear this . . . but the other place I felt a sense of elsewhere was in the camps. You have to remember that the first time I ever left Rhodes was when they took us to Athens and from Athens through Europe by train. I looked out the window, I watched the stations flash by: here was the continent I'd dreamt about for so long. And afterward . . . afterward in the camps themselves, we met the French women and Madame Katz and Paula, who were from Belgium. They spoke about Paris, Lyon, Brussels. They had actually seen and experienced, or were connected to, the places I had longed to know and to visit. They'd lived there. They were *from* there, *of* there . . ."

Under the unlikeliest of circumstances, the wider world came closer.

33

After the Italians came: this is a refrain that increasingly runs through Stella's conversation and introduces changes that took place in two periods, which may be politically distinct but experientially, and in her memory, tend to blur together.

The first period began in 1912, when the Italians won Rhodes in the Italo-Turkish War, and the second roughly ten years later, in 1923, when with the Second Treaty of Lausanne Italy established sovereignty over the Dodecanese and amplified their commitment to the region. (The Dodecanese, or "twelve islands," are actually fifteen larger and one hundred fifty smaller islands in the Eastern Aegean, many of them uninhabited, and in addition to Rhodes include Kos, Patmos, and Leros.)

The story of the Italian conquest of and rule over Rhodes—an island to which the country had no particular connection since ancient times—has been told in detail by Nathan Shachar and Esther Fintz Menascé, among others. It was wrapped up in Italy's yearning to compete with more established European countries by acquiring colonies (they would end up with Libya and Ethiopia in Africa), and it was part of a complex vying for and rebalancing of power in the region that erupted as the Ottoman Empire was being disbanded. But what did it *feel* like to Stella's family, and the community at large, to have their own immediate world metamorphose in this way?

After the Italians came—

They brought electricity and running water to the Juderia, where formerly most everyone drew their water from wells and public fountains.

They paved and renamed roads, restored and repurposed structures originally put up by the Knights.

They introduced modern medical care, early on offering free treatment to patients in the Juderia—as during the Spanish flu of 1918—and later built a modern hospital.

They granted citizenship to children born after the ratification of the Treaty of Lausanne.

Under the Ottomans, Jews and Turks lived and often worked together within the walled city and Greeks lived outside; after the Italians came, citizens were free to live where they chose.

The Italians inserted clunky Fascist-style modernist buildings into the medieval city; redesigned in fantasy Moorish style the springs at Kallithea outside the city; built and illuminated the Mandrakio; overhauled the port (with personal consequences for Stella's father) and removed the Turkish souk. They built a theater (the Teatro Puccini), a cinema (the San Giorgio), luxury hotels (the Albergo delle Rose), a social club (the Circolo d'Italia), schools, public buildings, private houses, and private villas—all rapidly and in the years just before Stella was born and during her childhood and youth.

As part of an antimalarial campaign, they drained swamps. They planted forests and established sophisticated methods of agriculture. In order to encourage tourism they excavated ruins from antiquity and installed an archaeological museum in a former hospital built by the Knights.

They required a permit for the whitewashing of the buildings in the Juderia that took place each year before Passover. They overhauled the educational system. They introduced buses and taxis, which (eventually) replaced carriages and mules, though both still came and went in the Juderia well into Stella's life. By 1936 they populated the island with many thousands of Italians, thereby changing the complexion of local society.

They introduced fashion, cinema, Italian literature, popular and classical music, sport (GER—Gioventù Ebraica di Rodi—was the Jewish soccer team), food (though the gastronomy of the Juderia held steady), and what might be described as an attitude, or mentality, that was decidedly more modern, forward- and western-looking and inadvertently facilitated a liberalizing of the habits and mores of the Jewish community. This was particularly true of members of the younger generation, who gradually stopped attending synagogue on Saturday mornings and even, on that very day, dared to venture to the beach, but eventually extended to the generation of Stella's parents, at least to some of the women, like Miriam, who began taking Saturday strolls with her friends outside of the Juderia, or went to the beach or to see a movie, or walked as far as Rodino, the verdant park half an hour outside the city walls that was the source of the sweet water everyone drank at the end of Yom Kippur. All of this would have been unheard of before the Italians came.

After Stella lays all this out for me, I ask her whether she thinks some, or most, of this modernizing might have happened no matter what, as even life in remote Rhodes pushed its way farther into the twentieth century. Wasn't this kind of gradual but inexorable change unfolding elsewhere in the southern Mediterranean and the Middle East during these same years?

She answers by pointing out the one thing that would not have happened no matter what: when the Italians came they also, if unwittingly, set in motion a series of events that would in time lead to the destruction of this same community, which had lived in relative peace in Rhodes for nearly half a millennium.

34

Under the Italians, Rhodes was governed by a variety of different men. Among the better ones—at least as perceived from the inevitably limited point of view of the young Stella—was one of the first, Mario Lago (November 1922 to November 1936), who oversaw many of the more ambitious building and restoration projects, transformed the seaside, overhauled the educational system, and persuaded Mussolini to approve the establishment of a rabbinical college in Rhodes, a gesture that was less enlightened and generous, though, than it might at first seem, considering that the Fascist leadership understood how useful it could be to train future rabbis who would scatter through the Levant and might be sympathetic to the regime. (Indeed, it has been suggested that separating out the island's Jews from the Greeks and Turks and giving them this kind of apparently favored treatment was part of the government's not-always-subtle way of dividing in order to consolidate their own power over these distinct but previously, for the most part, compatible communities.)

Lago was replaced by his antithesis, Cesare De Vecchi (December 1936 to December 1940). A hard-line Fascist and one of Mussolini's Quadrumvirs (the four men who helped propel Mussolini into office by organizing the Blackshirt march on Rome in October 1922), De Vecchi was a difficult personality whose posting to Rhodes as governor of the Dodecanese was effectively a banishment. Arrogant, mustached, and dogmatic, he began by reassuring the students of the rabbinical college that the institution was not in any danger ("I can assure you that Italy could not be imperial if she did not respect the religious beliefs of all the people living under her protective shield"); scarcely two years later he shuttered its doors ahead of the promulgation of the first racial laws, which he went on to enforce rigorously, adding some gratuitously nasty gubernatorial decrees of his own.

Even before the racial laws, though, there was a change, Stella says, in the atmosphere of Rhodes. "It was subtle but oppressive. It was a feeling. I think it had to do with the way, at first, small shops were closed or reconstructed and the Turkish bazaar was taken down and many of the minarets sliced off. De Vecchi wanted Rhodes to be elegant, modern, Italian. Before, you see, we lived—well, my grandmothers and parents lived—*a la turka*."

What did it mean exactly, I ask her, to live *a la turka*?

Stella laughs at this question, as though the answer should be so obvious to me by now, but then she reminds me, first, how deeply Turkish her parents' lives were. Her father, in his clothes (up to a certain period), language, and general sensibility, was in many ways essentially Turkish. He had strong professional connections to Turkey, including (in one aspect of his business) a Turkish partner, Husnu—Yehuda in fact never quite got over his mistrust of the Italians, whose presence on the island he regarded as temporary. Miriam was friends with Husnu's wife, Mervish, and on Saturdays used to take the girls to picnic with them at their *guerta*, their garden, which had a vegetable patch, just outside the city (like most Turkish and Jewish families, they lived within the walls). Turks not only brought them that post-fast pure water from Rodino, but daily yogurt and fruit and vegetables from their farms, and many of the Levis' neighbors in the Juderia had originally come from, or had deep roots in, places like Istanbul, Bodrum, and İzmir.

But when Stella speaks about living *a la turka* in this way, she is referring to what it felt like to live in a small community on a small island far from a big city, under the lingering influence of old—and old-fashioned—customs and habits. It was the opposite to living *a la franca*—like the Europeans. It meant, if you were a woman of an earlier generation, like Stella's grandmother Mazaltov, never venturing out of the neighborhood. It meant taking off your shoes before you walked into a room where there were rugs and sitting, often, on the floor with cushions; or fitting out your living room with a sofa built into three walls and upholstered, as the Levis' was, and instead sitting there. It meant wearing a fez to work (Stella's father—until his children made him stop) or a djellaba in the house and, if you were elderly, staying home and brewing and drinking chai (her grandmother Mazaltov again). It meant (if you were a woman of a certain age, or sometimes also a man of that age) never bathing in the sea. To the young people living *a la turka* was shorthand for being behind the times: "We used to make fun of my parents, we would say, '*Basta a la turka!*' "

Make fun of—while also rebelling against? "Well, I suppose it gave us, yes, the vocabulary that every new generation looks for, a way to distinguish ourselves, be separate . . . independent," Stella says reflectively. "But at the same time, you know, we could also mean *a la turka* in a positive way: as when Selma played the oud, which she learned from her Turkish teacher, or when we dressed up for Purim in a beautiful velvet gown that was embroidered in gold thread—that too was *a la turka*, as it was to serve baklava and other delicious sweets for holidays."

Month by month, year by year, these lingering traces of the old world began to recede, almost as if the sea itself were changing its rhythm and patterns. In Stella's memory the changes coincide with her grandmothers'

deaths in the mid-1930s, though in truth they were set in motion a long time before, as change generally is. Buildings were altered or repurposed, habits relaxed, and the sense of ease in one's own place—an at-home-ness on the island—altered too. Stella, for instance, remembers more than once having to stop and stand to attention when De Vecchi's motorcade went by: "In view of what came afterward it was a small thing, but at the time we didn't experience it that way." If Miriam, she says, found out that one of her girls didn't do what was expected, and got the family into difficulty with the government, she would have fainted, she would have had one of her famous migraines, or worse. Even Victor, who was politically engaged, an anti-Fascist with communist leanings and the most outspoken member of the family, said it was better, under the circumstances of the moment, to obey authority, and so obey Stella did. "I might have saluted De Vecchi," she says, "but I was never for a moment afraid of him—or anyone else for that matter. At least not then."

35

De Vecchi's reach was nevertheless deep and pernicious. Beyond his add-ons to the racial laws and what might be seen as relatively minor-key edicts, such as changing street names to those of famous Fascists (via del Duce, via Arnaldo—Benito's brother—Mussolini), under De Vecchi two particularly disturbing events took place.

The first was personal to Stella's family. As part of the rehabilitation of the Porta Santa Caterina, De Vecchi requisitioned the warehouse from which Yehuda, like his father before him, had conducted his business. In his impatience to modernize Rhodes, De Vecchi did this kind of thing regularly and widely: he simply wiped away (as did also, to be fair, some of his predecessors) any structure that was inconsistent with his plan to clean up and improve the island or restore it to an idealized version of its more glorious past. The relocation of his business was deeply unsettling to Stella's father, who had to move farther into the city.

The other change De Vecchi made affected the entire community. In order to install new public gardens, he ordered the Jewish cemetery moved from where it had stood for half a millennium. This occasioned some of the greatest grief Stella had felt, and seen, to that point in her life—not her grief personally so much as the grief of her parents, her family, the whole community. The disinterring of the bodies went on for weeks and was accompanied by religious ceremonies. In some cases the graves were unmarked because the traditional year had not yet passed since the dead person was buried; others bore stones that dated to the sixteenth century and were no longer legible. For weeks, then months, a heaviness hung over the Juderia; the neighborhood was never quite the same afterward.

"Even then some people were whispering in secret, 'It's a bad omen. You'll see.'"

"Did you believe them?" I ask Stella.

She shakes her head. "But we should have."

36

It was our own little piece of the earth.
Stella has said this to me before, more than once.
It was our own little piece of the earth—
Today she adds
—until they took it away from us.

The first thing they took away from Stella along with all the other Jewish children on the island was their right to go to school. To the young girl who kept that suitcase by the door, who was eager to do as well as her older sister Felicie, who competed with Silvia Rozio for the gold medal, who understood from an uncommonly early age what education meant, where it might lead, and who it might turn her into, this law hit her, as she phrases it, like a physical blow.

"In the fall of 1938 I was fifteen, and I was ready to begin *prima liceo*," she tells me. "I'd been waiting for this day for *years*. I experienced this banishment as a loss of something very personal. I lost the right to be human. I don't know if I can even talk about it."

Stella doesn't know if she can even talk about it, but once she begins, it's difficult for her to stop. Felicie, she says, with all her reading, with her love of history, used to speak about their ancestors' expulsion from Spain. It wasn't as if they'd ever forgotten. The families in the Juderia spoke a different language, they had their own cuisine, their superstitions and cures, their proverbs and songs. They knew that, in the past, the distant past, they had been kicked out of their homes, their countries, their schools. "But now we lived in the modern world," she says, her voice rising, accelerating. "We'd lived in Rhodes for five hundred years, for the past twenty-five years under these cultivated Italians who had brought us books, stylish clothes, who had imported opera, movies—Shirley Temple!" Like her classmates, Stella was a good *piccola Italiana*, obediently dressing in a pleated skirt, white shirt, and a foulard around her neck in order to entertain the governor with the other schoolchildren at the stadium. They divided the students into formations that spelled out *DUX* and *REX*; Stella was part of *REX*. "I was proud to stand up at the top of the curve of the *R*. We paraded like all the Catholic children, we were little Fascist patriots, and then suddenly we were *nothing*. They turned us into nonentities."

I listen as Stella tries to find a way to place this development in her young life. She describes her own sense of inferiority, something that haunted her for many decades afterward. She used to think it passed down to her from her mother, who felt in some ways lesser than her rich relations, or that it had something to do with being the last born of so many older, vibrant siblings. But then, she says, she sees herself marching across town to the *suore*, brimming with energy and curiosity and ambition; at home eavesdropping on her big sisters and perfecting her French by listening to them; at the beach listening to the boys talk, trying to understand what it was they talked *about*, and how they thought, and what they felt. "This is not the behavior of a person who feels inferior. Now

I've come to see that it had to do with what happened to me in 1938. The world around me changed—and, without choosing to, without wanting to, so did I."

37

Sometime after this conversation, I attend a series of lectures by Michele Sarfatti, a leading scholar of the racial laws in Italy, and Stella, unsurprisingly, is there too, as always sitting upright, watchful and patient, but with a patience that is taut, catlike, and vigilant. Upstairs at Casa Italiana, in the same room where Stella and I first met, Sarfatti carefully lays out, over the course of three evenings, the results of a lifetime of study and research, of extracting data from old archives and files, of building, figure by figure, fact by fact, a portrait of what it meant to be a Jew in Italy, or in an Italian possession like Rhodes, under Mussolini.

As I take notes, I watch Stella out of the corner of my eye. I wonder how it feels, eighty-plus years later, for her to hear the experiences she lived through recapped impersonally, as part of the historical record like this.

Halfway through the third evening Sarfatti comes to 1938 and the years immediately following:

> *In the fall and winter of 1938, the racial laws were promulgated.*

> *Only one public protest against the racial laws has surfaced, in a magazine published in Torino. In Napoli in September of 1938, street cleaners found little pieces of paper that said "stop racism." That was it.*

> *Jews were fired from all public employment, as soldiers, bus drivers, librarians.*

Jewish actors and performers were expelled from concert halls, theaters, film companies. Their names were expunged from recordings.

Jewish lawyers, physicians, and midwives were expelled or limited as to their work.

Jews were barred from being street vendors, hotelkeepers, circus artists, stationers, vendors of Catholic sacred objects.

In 1938, A Night at the Opera—*the Marx Brothers movie from 1935—was banned.*

In 1938, all traces of Judaism were stripped from schools: teachers, students, Jewish authors, mentions of Jewish authors in reference books; Spinoza, for example, was no longer mentioned. Marx, Einstein, Freud were wiped from textbooks, publishers stopped printing new books by Jewish authors, and older books by authors like Henri Bergson were confiscated and withdrawn from the market.

At the mention of Henri Bergson, a favorite of Felicie's, Stella's back stiffens. From where I am sitting I cannot see her face.

On the following Saturday Stella reminds me that the racial laws weren't just an installment in a history book, or part of a professor's research, to *her.* Under the racial laws her father was constrained to sell his wood and coal business to a new—Italian—owner, effectively becoming the man's employee. They did less and less business and took in less and less money. The family's finances began to undergo an alarming downturn.

She pauses for a moment then goes on to tell me about the year she went, on the anniversary of the racial laws, to speak to a class of schoolchildren.

"Imagine if someone told you this morning that your father could no longer run his own business and then, this afternoon, that you could no longer go to school," she said to them. "It would take you a lifetime to understand what that meant to your sense of who you are, what you deserve in life. I am what I am today because of what happened to me in 1938. I took it very personally. It felt like my family and I were being treated like animals—animals don't need to work or study, do they?"

Six years later when she was sent to Auschwitz, Stella could at least *see* the enemy: "You knew what you were up against, you knew what you had to do to survive. You learned how to fight for your life. When I was kicked out of school, the enemy was not visible. Who was I to fight against? I had no idea."

38

One day not long after the racial laws went into effect, Stella went to check out the new arrivals in Barbera's bookshop, which stood outside the Juderia but was still within the city walls. The local library at the Dante Alighieri had been closed by the new laws, depriving everyone in the neighborhood of access to books. That left Barbera, which was staffed by Rosa Galante, the *très sympa vendeuse* who was still able to work, for the moment, despite being Jewish herself.

Stella didn't have much money to buy many books, but she did love to look at them: *Gone with the Wind*. The latest novel from Hungary or Italy or France. In the bookshop this particular afternoon, also browsing, was a thoughtful man, thin, older—as in his early thirties older—whom Rosa Galante introduced to Stella: Luigi Noferini, the professor of Italian literature at the boys' high school (this was the companion to the girls' school, also established by the Italians, and run by the Padri Salesiani, though not all the instructors were priests). Noferini asked Stella what she was doing about studying now, given what had happened.

"Nothing," Stella said. "Reading, I guess. Waiting. Though I would *like* to do more . . ."

Standing there among the stacks of books, Stella and Noferini spoke for a while, and then Noferini made a proposal. What if, he said, he were able to put together a shadow school in the afternoons when he had finished teaching? He, and maybe also a handful of colleagues, could meet in secret with the Jewish students who were interested in pursuing their studies so that they might stay on track for—well, for the future.

He wouldn't want any payment, he told Stella. It was simply the right thing to do.

Noferini for literature; Professor Bianchi for Latin and Ancient Greek; Professor Sotgiu, the *Sardo*, for philosophy; a young man from the Juderia, Hugno, banished from school now himself, enlisted as math tutor: for the next few years these classes, held in the professors' homes, would end up replacing high school for Stella and five boys from the neighborhood.

Why no other girls? "I asked, but none of them wanted to join."

One evening, after the second lesson, Noferini asked Stella to stay behind. "Stella," he told her, "you have a very strong brain, but you have to promise to work hard. It would be a pity not to use it. You have to be prepared to keep up with the work we're going to give you, because this war will end soon and all this antisemitism will go away, and then you will go to university, I know it. Do you promise?"

She promised.

Almost from the beginning Stella understood that Noferini personified all the things she longed to know, and longed to be. He loved literature, history, and music. A gifted tenor, he took singing lessons from a local teacher. Some of the first arias she ever heard, from *La Gioconda* and *La Fanciulla del West*, she heard in his voice; she wouldn't see the operas staged until a lifetime later.

He had strong opinions on poetry. He preferred the *Inferno* to the *Paradiso*, because he wasn't at all convinced that paradise existed. His syllabus included foreign writers like Tennyson and Ruskin; echoing Sister Teresa, he encouraged her to learn verse by heart.

In the late-afternoon light in her Greenwich Village living room, Stella can still, three-quarters of a century later, dip into that deep memory of hers and come up with an example from D'Annunzio: "*Non è mai tardi per tentare l'ignoto, non è mai tardi per andare più oltre.*"

"It's never too late to seek the unknown," she adds, translating into English. "Never too late to go beyond."

39

Reverberations from the racial laws were felt throughout the Juderia and touched different lives in different ways, not all of them expected, or predictable.

"It's true that I wept when I was kicked out of school," Stella says, "but in the end what could we do? I was lucky, or tenacious, however you choose to see it. I found a solution, at least to my education, at least temporarily. And anyway, we had to accept our new reality. In my mind, the acceptance was bound up in the Jews' ability to adapt. I'm not saying it was *good* to accept, but you have to go on living. So we went on living."

"But did you not—how to put this?—feel betrayed by these Italians, whom you had embraced so fully?" I ask her. "Or at the very least feel hurt, or troubled, by what they had done?"

Stella thinks for a moment. "You have to remember that I was fifteen. And I wasn't Felicie or Victor—I wasn't exactly politically attuned, not at that age. I think what I did was separate out the individual Italians I knew, people like the nuns who taught us and Noferini, from the Italian government. I thought of them as two different kinds of Italians. Individual people were one category, the government another. I don't believe I was alone in doing this either."

The Levis went on living, even if it meant the beginning of the end for her father—the end of his work, that is, because first, under the racial laws, he lost control of his business; and then because Victor was so inflamed by this development that Yehuda had to arrange for him to move to Congo (a costly but potentially lifesaving decision, as it turned out); and finally because the racial laws coincided with Yehuda's advancing diabetes, which eventually made it impossible for him to continue to work at all. I ask Stella if the laws contributed to his poor health. "How do you separate the one from the other? They issued the laws; his business struggled; he became ill; we fell on hard times—*very* hard times."

After a moment she continues: "But we made do. We . . . coped. That is what you would say in America. What choice did we have?"

As Renée had at least finished school at the *terza tecnica*, the equivalent of middle school that prepared students for office work, rather than the rigorous high school (Felicie's—and later Stella's) that preceded university, Miriam encouraged her to find a job, and she did, in the office of the lawyer San Pietro.

"I'll tell you something that happened after the racial laws that you might not expect," Stella says. "We, what remained of the youth of the Juderia, being forbidden, at least for a time, from socializing with the Italians, or frequenting the places the Italians frequented, turned inward. There were fewer of us, and we grew closer, as a group, becoming friends with people of different ages, gathering on the stairs in front of the old Alhadeff home and deepening our conversations, our connections, and our bonds."

And as they often did in Rhodes, matters unfolded in their own particular way. Even with De Vecchi's stringent add-ons to the racial laws, eventually some of the laws were not so rigorously upheld. Jews, banished from going to the cinema, eventually returned. Forbidden from going to the beach, they managed to slip back there too. It was illegal, at first, for Jews to consult non-Jewish doctors, but in time that rule, as well, broke down—Stella, with her excellent Italian, she reminds me, accompanied the father of Nisso Cohen to the hospital where he was seen by Dottore Galina.

The rabbinical college was closed. Despite the complex intentions that may have lay behind its establishment, there was no avoiding heartbreak at the closing of that very special institution, just as there was no way to ignore the fact that *Il Messaggero di Rodi*, the Italian paper, was beginning to spike its coverage of local life with unvarnished anti-Jewish sentiment and language (*"All'inferno tutti gli Ebrei"*—To hell with all Jews—read a headline on the eve of Yom Kippur, 1938), or to reverse the law that forbade Jews from owning radios (even if it was disobeyed), or starting or continuing their businesses, and all the rest.

Odd, bizarre, even brutal things happened that seemed to come out of nowhere: Stella's classmate Evelina Menasce's father, John—*"Jean*, we called him, *à la Française"*—was for a time president of the Jewish community, and he decided one evening in early 1939 to host a dinner for some of the local Fascist grandees. He didn't merely set his table with knives; he employed a butler and several housemaids who lived in and served this meal and made an impression, the wrong impression, it turned out: a few days later he was called in by one of his dinner guests (or so the story went) and was compelled to drink a quantity of *olio di ricino*—castor oil—and then forced to run several laps around the stadium. "And you can imagine what happened after that."

The following morning Menasce's Italian partner put him on a private airplane. *"Boom*, he was whisked off to Paris, and soon the whole family followed, the wife, all three children, Evelina and the two others. They all ended up in Buenos Aires."

What was his crime, exactly, I ask Stella.

"Exactly, I cannot tell you. He was a Jewish banker who had done well and lived well and employed the services of a butler and had invited the wrong people to dinner at the wrong time. Possibly that, in that place, and at that moment, was enough. But it was a sign, one of several that we were beginning to take note of by then."

The change in atmosphere infiltrated even the secret school, when during lessons one evening at Sotgiu's house the professor opened the window and noticed something small and metallic in the corner of the sill that he'd never seen before. He touched it, tugged on it, worked it loose: a microphone. The house was being bugged. "Sotgiu was an opponent of the regime, so probably already on the government's radar,"

Stella explains. His wife came running in and anxiously asked, "What shall we do? Should you stop giving these lessons? What if we get into trouble?"

"Let them listen," Sotgiu calmly answered. "Maybe these Fascists will learn a little philosophy. Maybe it will help open up their minds . . ."

There is one clear area where racial laws unintentionally spared some people's lives. An especially thorny provision revoked the rights of Jews who had come to Rhodes (or, on the mainland, to Italy in general) after January 1919; these "foreigners" were instructed to leave the island by March 1939, which meant that somewhere around five hundred people were compelled to sell their businesses and houses, pack up their belongings and lives, and move elsewhere. They landed in Tangiers, Palestine, the Belgian Congo, Rhodesia, and South America, places where, as it turned out, they were spared deportation to the camps.

L'ebreo errante, the wandering Jew, by choice or by decree—usually by decree: "Sometimes," Stella says dryly, "this has been our salvation, after all."

40

She was not an experienced young woman, and it crept up on her. She was aware—she had read Charlotte Brontë—that between teacher and pupil, especially an older man and a younger woman, there could be an energy, a dynamic. During the first years of their secret school, when Stella was fifteen, then sixteen, she and Noferini remained merely teacher and pupil, pupil and teacher, but at seventeen . . . at seventeen one evening they were sitting alone side by side at his desk. They had finished their lessons for the day. Stella closed her book, and Noferini put his hand on hers. Just that; no more. "And there was that *frisson* again, for the second time in my life. The *frisson* was followed by a chill. It flashed through me, head to toe . . ."

Afterward Noferini offered to walk her to the door to the old city, since he lived outside and she, of course, within the ancient walls. They spoke about literature the whole time. Literature and poetry, not what had happened at his desk. When they said good-bye, he blushed.

I ask Stella if she remembers how this moment made her feel.

"It didn't matter what his age was. And after all this was another—another time. He never crossed a line. I didn't feel taken advantage of. He was my teacher, and now he became my friend, more than my friend."

"More than your friend . . ."

"Not in the way you think," she says. "Not then." She pauses. "Luigi wasn't young, he wasn't especially handsome, but he interested me. And I appear to have interested him. After that everything felt, well, *different*."

41

Noferini became Stella's friend and more than her friend and part of her circle of friends, as she became part of his. One day he said to her, "There's someone you simply have to meet, a lawyer who is a lieutenant in the Italian army here. He is one of the finest people I've ever been lucky to know."

Noferini had met Lieutenant Gennaro Tescione, a Neapolitan lawyer from a family of distinguished lawyers, at the Circolo d'Italia, once a social club for all people of a certain class in Rhodes, now reinvented as a gathering place for officers and professionals and their families from which, after 1938, Jews were excluded. Tescione was younger than Noferini, in his late twenties, and he reminded Stella, once they were introduced, of Felicie: he was something of an anachronism, a man with a heart and soul more suited to the mid-nineteenth century than to the early twentieth. He had old-fashioned ideas about military (and lawyerly) duty and responsibility. He referred to women, unfailingly, as *Signora* or *Signorina*—for the longest time even she was *Signorina Stella*—whereas Noferini was far more down to earth, one of them. He wrote romantic

poetry. He gave Stella a book and inscribed in it, evoking Dante, "*Nel cammino della mia vita sarai sempre un'immagine di luce*"—Along the path of my life you will always be a beacon of light.

Tescione was a man of principle: in his spare time he took on, and won, an impressive pro bono case for a local Greek man who had been accused of rebelling against the Italian regime. He was athletic—a swimmer, like Stella, and unlike Noferini. He helped her learn the crawl, which had just come to Rhodes. He taught her to streamline her dive off the *trampolino*, the diving board that floated offshore on a platform. One afternoon, when they had swum far out, beyond all the other swimmers, just the two of them in the cool cobalt sea, he paused mid-stroke. "Do you think we could make it all the way to Turkey?" he wondered, laughing, giddy—or so it struck Stella in the moment. Now, looking back, she revisits this question of Tescione's and wonders if his laugh wasn't so much giddy as nervous, whether perhaps he was actually exploring the idea with her, asking, could we, if things turn bad, perhaps save our lives by swimming as far as the Turkish coast?

Before long Stella realized there was much *simpatia* between them too.

She came to understand certain things about herself that same summer:

"It was the year, the summer, that I first felt *free*—that I could *be* free. Free to do what I wanted, free of worrying that people might say, 'Oh, Stella, she takes lessons from one Italian man and goes swimming with another.' And people *did* speak about me, but it meant nothing, I decided it meant nothing. I think my mother was a help. She welcomed Luigi to our house. She knew I was friends with Gennaro—she even sent food to him when he fell ill. She understood, in a way that was quite modern I now see, really quite amazing, that these Italians had a powerful attraction for many of us girls in the Juderia. She was open and trusting of me. She trusted me in my friendships with these two Italian men."

Her mother said something that summer that Stella never forgot. A young woman in the Juderia, poor, had gone out with an Italian soldier and became pregnant. Everyone in the young woman's family went into mourning; tongues wagged up and down the streets of the neighbor-hood. Miriam, who was already avidly opposed to all kinds of gossip, said, "No one who has a daughter should ever open her mouth on a subject like this." And in the Levi house no one did.

42

One afternoon from the terrace of La Rotunda a man began tossing apricots down toward the beach where Stella, her friend Clara Gabriel, and Michel Menasce, who lived on Kos but was visiting Rhodes, had gone for a swim. Looking back, Stella feels this fellow must have known one of the other people there, Michel most probably. Who, as the tallest of them, caught the tossed fruit? Stella, of course. The man laughed; Stella and her friends laughed. The man came down off the terrace and introduced himself.

Renzo Rossi was in his late thirties, a successful businessman and entrepreneur, university-educated and with a wide-ranging interest in books, music, antiquities, and history. He had come to Rhodes at the suggestion of his brother-in-law, with whom he shared a house in town while he engaged a Swiss architect to build him a handsome villa in the countryside near Trianda, where he cultivated grapes—wine was just one of his enterprises (his vineyard, CAIR, is still producing today). Before long he and Stella became friends, good friends.

A *third* older Italian man?

"You still haven't understood my character yet, Michael," she tells me. "I was outside of the usual way of doing things. I was open to all friendships, with men, with women. With people of all backgrounds and all ages. You don't have to go to bed with everyone who interests you, certainly not then you didn't, not there. It wasn't that I had this attitude consciously. It was just how I was, how I lived."

Before long Stella introduced Rossi to Noferini and Tescione, and Rossi often invited them all to Sunday lunch at his new villa, along with the San Pietro sisters, who worked for him, and other lively young and not-so-young people. He employed a Greek woman, Evangelina, who cooked beautifully. For Stella's nineteenth birthday he bought her a bicycle, a Bianchi, in *bluette*, a gift that surprised her a little but that she accepted, because it was a practical gift, logical in the context in which they found themselves living, since having a bicycle made it so much easier to come and go from the Juderia.

Eventually it emerged that Rossi was Jewish, something Stella realized when she noticed that, while he continued to administer his businesses, their ownership had been officially transferred to his Catholic brother-in-law. "We had no idea. He seemed perfectly Italian, whatever that means. He never came to the Juderia to attend synagogue; he didn't care about such things. But apparently he was from an old Jewish family in Tuscany."

Was he looking for a wife? I ask Stella. And was she, perhaps, a candidate?

"Maybe I was," she says evasively, "maybe I wasn't."

Her eyes are sparkling. I feel that there is a story here, but I've learned by now to be patient.

"What I liked about Rossi was his conversation, his cultivation," she adds. "I liked being treated as a full-fledged adult at his lunches—certainly I tried to *be* one! He took an interest in our secret school, in what Noferini and the other professors were doing with us. I wonder now if, being Jewish, he was trying to imagine what he would have done in our place. His interest and curiosity were very appealing. The whole way he thought and lived, it was a taste, for me, of the kind of life I dreamed of having."

43

In one state of mind Stella speaks about accommodating herself to the new reality in the years following the racial laws; in another she offers a different take on that same experience. Very likely both were true, or true at different times.

The different take:

"Quite honestly, I am what I am from the racial laws. Being kicked out of school was the greatest possible humiliation, as I've told you. This experience formed me, you might say malformed me."

She goes on to explain that she still, to this day, feels inferior to most people she knows. Even when she worked, she struggled to assert herself, to advocate for her rights. She helped other people make money but, for a long time, didn't do as much for herself in that regard as she might have. She failed to see projects, plans, ambitions through.

The pattern repeated itself over and over. She took guitar lessons, but by the third one, not having mastered the instrument, she gave up. She took lessons in English diction but lasted scarcely a month. She enrolled in a creative writing class at Columbia University. The professor read her first assignment, a sketch of her life, and said, "Stella you have fantastic ideas and you have to develop them—I will help you"; Stella reacted by deciding she wasn't a writer. She was too impatient; she couldn't stick with difficult or exasperating projects; she wanted everything to come immediately and easily. Later on she went to NYU to study psychology. "I stayed with it until it was time to do the exam, and then I panicked."

At the word *exam* I notice Stella's face alter, take on a hardness that looks very much like pain. And she notices me noticing.

"There's something that happened, that has to do with my education . . ."

She pauses. She looks at the wall of books to her right, then at the photograph of her mother hanging on one wall, then to the far end of the room, where there are more books still.

"The professors who were teaching us—Noferini, Sotgiu, Bianchi— they discovered that, even though we had been forbidden from attending school, we were still eligible, if you can believe this, to sit for the *maturità*—the exam that would permit them to attend university—"and so we agreed to. *I* agreed to. I studied, let's just say, intensely. I knew the material, I knew the answers. I was prepared. Believe me, I was."

The exams were being given at the *scuola maschile*. The examiners were the priest-teachers at the boys' school, and when she stepped into the room, the first classroom she'd been inside of in two years, and saw them all lined up behind a table, looking at her, waiting for her, Stella stumbled. Worse: she lost her way. "I froze. It was like one of those anxiety dreams where you open your mouth to scream, and no sound comes out."

No sound came out, yet she was fully awake. Not a syllable, not a phrase. She knew the material, but she could not take the exam. She could not *begin* the exam.

Stella's face, when she finishes describing this day to me, is not so much troubled as utterly without expression. Frozen, remote.

"Later on in my life, when I thought of that moment, that scene, I likened it to the Spanish Inquisition—my own little Spanish Inquisition," she continues. "Only *I* was responsible. For the rest of my life, this failure stayed with me. Haunted me. Even when I was in America, even when I lived in New York, and was happy, I knew that I was a failure in life. I have come to see that it was because of—or I have come to believe, or tell myself, that it was in part because of—that day when I couldn't open my mouth, when I couldn't speak the answers that were all there, in my head."

But didn't her experience at the exam happen in a particular context and under circumstances that were beyond her control? A failure in life: isn't this a bit . . . sweeping, or absolute?

When I ask Stella this, she ponders for a moment, then says, "Not to me."

44

With the war, which Italy joined on the side of the Axis in June 1940, another sort of elsewhere altogether was introduced to the island as refugees from Europe began arriving, a flow of people who were determined, no matter what, to reach Palestine. It turns out that the waters of the Dodecanese had more emigrant boats sailing through them than Stella had any idea, but she came to understand who these people were and where they were heading after the appearance of two memorable vessels, both of which left a distinct impression on her and the community at large.

The first was the *Rim*, flying—like many of these vessels—a Panamanian flag when it set out from Costanţa on the Black Sea, carrying six hundred Jews from Czechoslovakia, Austria, Hungary, and Romania; arriving in Rhodes in June 1939, it picked up another two hundred passengers, many of them those "foreign" Jews resident on the island, meaning those who had arrived after January 1919 and were to have left by the spring of 1939. Shortly after sailing, though, the *Rim* caught fire on July 3 near Symi, and under De Vecchi's orders the Italian navy successfully rescued all 814 passengers and thirteen crew members, who were brought back to Rhodes, put up in a makeshift encampment in the soccer stadium, and fed and looked after, in part by residents of the Juderia, before setting off again for Palestine on August 13.

Stella's upstairs neighbor Rebecca Leon was among the Rhodeslis who were not required but chose to leave. When Stella asked her how she came to this decision, Rebecca answered that she was a Zionist and saw the future in Palestine, not in Rhodes.

Rebecca was not a lone Zionist in her generation, which was maybe half a generation above Stella's: "There were meetings, there were talks, there were Zionist and revisionist debates—you heard the names Jabotinsky and Trumpeldor and Weizmann discussed passionately, especially among the young people—but it's not as if everyone picked up and left or even talked about picking up and leaving. Many more young people went to the Belgian Congo, Rhodesia, the States." She pauses. "You must remember though, I was the baby in the family. There was no possibility of *me* going anywhere."

More dramatic than the *Rim* was the improbable and downright cinematic voyage of the *Pentcho*, a Danube paddle steamer that set off from Bratislava under a Bulgarian flag in May 1940 with five-hundred-plus passengers who also hoped to reach Palestine. Held up for six weeks on the Dobra, the riverboat, which was never built to be seaworthy, managed to sail into the Black Sea that September. It survived storms, gales, and the interference of the British, who were trying to block Jewish immigration to the Holy Land, and nevertheless managed to cross the Bosporus, make it through the Dardanelles, and into the Aegean, arriving in Piraeus in time for the hopeful passengers to celebrate Rosh Hashana.

Setting off again toward the east, the *Pentcho* passed by the island of Stampalia, where an Italian tugboat directed it out of Italian territorial waters. A few days later, on October 9, the *Pentcho*'s boiler exploded and it went aground on Kamilanisi, a two-mile-long deserted rock, basically, where the passengers quickly disembarked, salvaged what food, provisions, and materials they could, and watched the vessel sink, leaving behind what one passenger described as a ragged red carpet that, as John Bierman reports in *Odyssey*, his lively book about the *Pentcho*, was made up of the profusion of bedbugs that tormented the travelers during the whole of their improbable journey.

The marooned *Pentcho* was spotted by a British ship and reported to the International Red Cross. Before long De Vecchi, whose governorship extended just barely to Kamilanisi, was given orders from Mussolini's chief of staff, Pietro Badoglio, to dispatch another rescue mission—no one wanted six hundred civilians dead on Italian territory. Once again a village's worth of European Jews were brought to the soccer stadium; there, and in the air force barracks where they were eventually lodged, they were fed (in a time of strained resources, meagerly fed) by members of the Juderia, Jewish relief organizations, and the local government, much to the displeasure of De Vecchi. In a telegram to his superiors he begged them to free him as soon as possible from these refugees, who, he claimed, were putting such a burden on the island. He also reached out to the governments involved (Germany and Slovakia) to ask them to come collect their citizens. After rescuing these Jews—if under orders—he was now trying to send them back to the dangers from which they had fled.

Fortunately, as it would turn out, none of these countries was interested in retrieving its citizens, who lived for more than a year on Rhodes in what was effectively imprisonment, with no jobs, clothes, education or toys for their children, and, worst of all, without any sense of what was going to happen to them.

Stella had a memorable personal experience with the *Pentcho*. Somehow she learned that there was an accomplished ophthalmologist among the passengers, and she decided to see if he would examine her father, who was slowly going blind from diabetes.

"I was that sort of person," Stella tells me when I say how impressed I am by the fact that, as a young woman, she was mature enough to think of this possible solution, in an improbable situation, to her father's health. She merely shrugs and says, "I was always looking for ideas, for new things to try. I loved my father. I would have done anything to help."

The physician spoke French, which made it easy for Stella to convey her request. He obtained permission to come to the Juderia, where he examined Yehuda. "I regret to tell you," he said, "that your father will without a doubt, over time, go blind. There's nothing to be done."

It was not easy news to hear, but Stella felt it was better to know than not to know.

By way of thanks, she invited the doctor's wife to the Turkish baths for an afternoon. The woman spoke fluent French and seemed modern, worldly. At the baths she took off all her clothes without hesitating and stood naked in front of these women she'd never met before. Afterward, Stella accompanied her back to the stadium.

In January of 1942, the fate of these passengers became clear when they were transferred to Ferramonti, an internment camp in Calabria. "We cried when they left," Stella recalls. "We thought they were heading into a grim, uncertain future." Instead they joined other foreign Jews and enemy aliens living in captivity in the camp and remained there until they were liberated by the Allies in September 1943.

45

At La Rotunda, the fancier of the two central beaches on the island, where for the moment no one seemed to mind that the Jews were again swimming, Stella stood in line at the foot of the diving board one afternoon the following summer, just behind a man she didn't recognize. He was dark and had an interesting air, though he didn't look Italian. Stella had no idea where he was from until he spoke, and she realized not only that he wasn't Italian but that he didn't speak or understand the language. She quickly ascertained that he was from Vienna, though, and spoke French.

The fellow told Stella that he worked for General Ulrich Kleemann, the German officer who had recently been posted to Rhodes.

Right away Stella said to him, "*Je suis juive.*"

He shrugged and said, "*Ça va.*"

She ran into this fellow several times at the beach that season, and every time he saw her he nodded at her affably. Once they even took a swim together, as though they were normal people meeting in a normal place at a normal time.

Not long afterward Stella attended a birthday party in the garden of her friend Stella Sidis's house outside of the Juderia. As was often their habit, after dinner the girls, in a variation of their mothers in the *kortijos*, gathered in a circle and began to sing. Only instead of the old Judeo-Spanish *kanzones*, they sang the modern music that they'd heard at the bandstands by the beach, or from records. One of their favorites that season was "Tornerai"—

> *Tornerai da me*
> *perché l'unico sogno sei del mio cuor*
> *tornerai*
> *tu perché senza i tuoi baci languidi*
> *non vivrò*

Before they finished, the young women realized that they had an audience: one by one a group of men, after-dinner drinks and cigars in hand, had wandered out onto a balcony belonging to the house next door, which overlooked the Sidis garden. Among them was Stella's acquaintance from the beach, and his superior, a man Stella took to be General Kleemann himself.

The general leaned over to Stella's acquaintance who, translating Kleemann's request, wondered if the girls knew the song also in French, the language in which it had become so popular.

Of course they did, Stella answered.

Would they sing it?

Pourquoi pas?—

> *J'attendrai*
> *Le jour et la nuit*
> *J'attendrai, toujours*
> *Ton retour . . .*

Next the German officers joined in—

> *Wo du auch bist (wo du auch bist)*
> *Oh, ich bin bei dir.*
> *Wen du auch küsst (wen du auch küsst)*
> *Oh, ich verzeih' dir*
> *Mach deinen Weg (mach deinen Weg)*
> *Und dann befrei mich.*
> *Komm zurück—lass mich nicht warten.*

When they finished: applause, all around. Kleemann smiled, thanked the girls, then went indoors.

46

The friendly, music-loving general under whose leadership these very young women he'd asked to sing would be deported to Auschwitz: Stella tells me this story several times over the years, and it's not hard to understand why. Yet it turns out that in her memory she has conflated two separate parties: Stella Sidis's birthday celebration (April 11, 1943) and the evening when the young women sang for the Germans (sometime between May of that year, when Kleemann assumed his post, and, most likely, the Passover bombings of April 1944). The conflation is not so interesting—but something that transpired at the first party most certainly is.

In 2011 the scholar Marco Clementi and Eirini Toliou, the director of the state archives in Rhodes, learned that hundreds if not thousands of old documents that had been sitting unexamined for nearly seven decades at the local police station were about to be tossed out to make space, and they were told to come deal with them right away or lose them forever. They went right away and found a masterwork of bureaucracy, what turned out to be more than ninety thousand sheets of paper in total, that chronicled the Italian administration of the island as far back as 1912. Among their many discoveries was a report written by an anonymous informant, Italian in all probability, who attended Stella Sidis's birthday party—as an invited guest, he (or she) must have been a friend or a friend of a friend—and then delivered his (or her) findings to the governor of the island.

"On the afternoon of Sunday, April 11th [1943]", the report begins,

> a citizen of the Jewish race, Stella Sidis, the unmarried daughter of Behor and Rebecca Hasson, born on Rhodes on April 14, 1919, and employed by the Commerciale, hosted a party to celebrate her birthday at 9, Via Vittorio Emanuele III.

The informant goes on to list the guests. A number of Italian soldiers were present, including, significantly, a certain Servizi, who is identified as a lieutenant to Gennaro Tescione—Tescione had just won his court case defending a Greek man of insurrection against the Italian government, which as a result did not regard the lawyer very favorably—and the young ladies whose names are given thus: Bice Sampietro, Cohen Vittoria, Notrica Sara, the sisters Stella and Renata Levi, the sisters Silvia and Sofia Alhadeff, Notrica Rachele, Sciaroon Lucia, and Ialussi Paraschevi. All are of the Jewish race, the writer notes, except for Sampietro, who was Catholic, and Ialussi, who was Orthodox.

> Sidis served the guests cookies, sesame crackers, candies, and vermouth. During the reception several records were played on a gramophone and people danced and listened to the radio.

No state secrets imparted, no revelations, no crimes, no infractions (even the radio, which after the racial laws, Jews were forbidden from owning, is carefully identified as belonging to Ernesto Licitri, Stella Sidis's Catholic brother-in-law); the account, on the surface, could not be more prosaic. What is astonishing about it is its very *existence* and the fact that this page is one of thousands found in the archives in which ridiculously, and, from this distance, poignantly, innocent details (the sesame crackers, the gramophone) attest to the surveillance apparatus the Fascist government had established in faraway Rhodes, with perhaps special focus on young women in the Jewish community who socialized with members of the Italian militia.

Stella and her friends were going about their lives without any inkling that their most casual encounters, movements, and conversations were being monitored, bugged (Sotgiu), preserved, and shared. (Surveillance wasn't limited to the Jews; Greek citizens of interest to the government were also being tracked.) Far more problematically, as it would turn out, their identities were known and recorded—theirs and every last member of the Jewish community, an act of bureaucratic diligence that would have irrevocable consequences for their lives in July of the following year.

47

I ask Stella a question—a version of the same question—five, six times on several Saturdays as we come closer to speaking about the events leading up to the deportation: In Rhodes, what did they know, what did they understand, about the war? And more specifically: What did they know, what did they understand, about what was happening to European Jews?

Always I receive a variation on the same answer:

The war was happening in faraway Europe.

Or:

Terrible things were happening to the Jews, but they were happening, it seemed, in another world.

Or:

A tragedy had beset the Ashkenazi, but who could possibly care about us, or even bother about us, living so far away in Rhodes?

Or:

Even when they deported the Jews from Salonika, fifty thousand of them, no one told us. Or the news was kept from us. We didn't hear it discussed on the BBC.

Once she says to me:

Maybe we didn't want to know. Couldn't let ourselves know.

Only once does she say this.

I do some reading.

I learn that as early as 1934, an article by Israel Cohen, *"Gli Ebrei in Germania"*—the Jews in Germany—circulated in the Juderia. In this piece Cohen accurately, and presciently, describes the persecution of German Jews being a tragedy of such scope and significance that it belonged to a category unto itself. He says that it was distinguished from all other modern political movements by its racial hatred. He says that it represented a return to the barbarism of the Middle Ages.

Over sixteen pages Cohen anatomizes the rise, origin, thinking, expression, and contagiousness of Germany's hatred of the Jews.

"We knew," Stella says when I report back.

I learn that in the mid-thirties there were protests on the island, many by the young, against Germany.

"There were," Stella says.

I learn that one of the rabbis suggested boycotting German goods.

"He did," Stella says.

Then she reminds me: "Remember, this was Germany everyone was concerned about. Rhodes was *not* Germany."

I collect and review some of the things Stella has previously told me about life on the island in this period—bracketed, say, by the promulgation of the racial laws in the fall of 1938; continuing through June 1940, when Italy entered the war; and extending almost to July 1943, when Mussolini was overthrown.

Already she has told me that they listened to the radio, even after listening to the radio was forbidden, and that the BBC's *Radio Londra* made it possible for them to follow the progression of the war. "But no one mentioned the camps on the radio," she makes it clear. "Not ever."

She has told me that in 1938 and 1939, and sometimes earlier, the richer Jewish families in Rhodes, the Menasces, the Notricas, the Alhadeffs, many of them by then living outside of the Juderia, read the signs, knew it was time to go, and left—for Paris, Tangiers, Egypt, and elsewhere.

She has told me that in her own family it was a relief when Selma (many of whose friends were ardent Zionists) married and set off for the States, where she was not in danger of getting into any kind of political trouble.

She has told me that Felicie knew, from reading in the newspaper, when Freud, who was one of her heroes, left Vienna for London in 1938;

Felicie knew, then, they all knew, that if Freud left his beloved home, it meant that elsewhere in Europe, not just Germany, life was now dangerous, very dangerous, for the Jews.

She has told me that Victor, the most politically aware member of the family, understood that the Italians were growing uncomfortably close to the Germans. She has told me that he was infuriated when Renée and Stella, like all the other schoolchildren, participated in the Fascist parades; she adds now that he hated colonialism too, hated it when the girls came home from school singing *Facetta Nera* ("Little Black Face")—

> *Faccetta nera, bell'Abissina*
> *Aspetta e spera che già l'ora si avvicina*
> *Quando staremo vicino a te*
> *Noi te daremo un'altra legge e un altro Re*

The marching song, which was written for the Second Italo-Ethiopian War, tells the story of how Italian soldiers will free a beautiful Abyssinian girl from slavery and give her a better life, and it drove Victor nuts.

For reasons both political and economic, Victor left (ironically, Stella points out from this distance, for another colony). And Felicie left, because clearly there was no viable life ahead for her in Rhodes. And yet the rest of the family did not go—though not, it turns out, for lack of trying. Joe Hasson, Yehuda's nephew, the son of his older sister Behora Rachel Hasson, offered to pay their passage to America, as Yehuda had originally paid for his, but the Americans would not issue the Levis visas, as even though they were down to four people there were too many of them in a single family.

The Levis tried to leave, for economic reasons and because the future had come to feel uncertain, not because they had any specific inkling of what lay ahead, which they didn't. Nor did the majority of the nearly 1,650 other members of their community. When it was still possible to leave, as it was, theoretically, until just days before the deportation, who would have stayed, if he or she had known what was coming? "No sane person," says Stella.

I bring up the *Rim* and the *Pentcho*, boatloads of Jews desperate to flee Europe who came to Rhodes and, in the case of the *Pentcho*, stayed there for more than a year, and interacted with the Rhodeslis, with Stella and her family specifically (the eye doctor, his wife): Did they never speak about the place they were fleeing from and why? "We knew why they had left their countries," Stella says. "We didn't feel the need to upset them further by asking probing questions. Again, what was going on was happening *there*, far away from us, from our world. It was happening to those Jews, not us Jews. And don't forget that the *Pentcho* left Europe well before the Nazis began to implement their 'final solution.'"

Still: the signs, the reports, the omens, the worries, the newspaper articles—while none of this was definitive, it wasn't exactly subtle. *What did you understand?* evolves into *Why didn't you understand?* I ask this gently; I am trying to see back, to see what the world looked and felt like to them, even after they had been deprived of their civil rights, even after they heard reports of German (and were confronted with more frequent examples of Italian) antisemitism, even after the apparently informed affluent families had left.

Calmly Stella answers: "Michael, you are looking back from a point of knowing. You must remember that. *We did not know.* Even as we were boarding the boats that took us away from Rhodes, we thought, *Oh, we're going to another island. We're going to a work camp. All this is temporary. We'll be back, of course we will.*"

48

On July 25, 1943, Mussolini was overthrown, and a provisional government was formed under Marshall Pietro Badoglio. Mussolini's portraits were summarily removed from local government offices, but for several months life on the island—certainly as Stella experienced it—felt unchanged, untouched; they remained far away from the center of action, as ever.

Then on September 8, 1943, Italy declared armistice with the Allies; three days later Rhodes was in the hands of the Germans.

How did this happen?

It probably helps to remember that, back in May 1939, with the Pact of Steel, Germany and Italy entered into a military and political alliance that remained intact all the way until Mussolini was deposed, and that just two months after he was removed from office, the Allies landed in Salerno in the south of Italy with the intention of pushing the Germans out of the country. The Germans, meanwhile, were prepared to invade Italy, which they did, capturing Rome in September 1943, the same month during which they also seized control of faraway Rhodes.

Every historian who tells the story of the three consequential days that would eventually doom the island's Jewish community emphasizes a different player, or turning point, or communication—or miscommunication. For Stella's cousin Esther Fintz Menascé, the governor of Rhodes at the time, World War I veteran Admiral Inigo Campioni, was too respectful and trusting of his recent ally and counterpart, Ulrich Kleemann. This was true even though Campioni had received a telegram from Rome urging him, as Nathan Shachar points out, to resist the Germans' attempt to disarm the "numerically superior, but technically inferior" Italian forces. (There were said to have been a lavish thirty-five thousand Italian troops stationed on the island in the fall of 1943 to about ten thousand German, though the latter were better equipped.) Menascé describes Campioni and Kleemann meeting and coming to a gentleman's agreement that they would keep their troops separate: "*Ich habe einen Kameraden gefunden*"—I have found a comrade—Kleemann apparently declared as he left the castle, only promptly afterward to order his men to attack the Italians according to a meticulous plan that appears to have long been in the works. (Another plan in the works, according to Marco Clementi, concerned the prospect of British action against Rhodes, first in 1940 to 1941 and again in 1943; both plans, he maintains, were resisted by the Americans, who considered the island of too little significance to bother about.)

The Germans pushed ahead; the Italians fought for three intense but brief days; lives were lost (the most reliable figures suggest ninety-one German and one hundred twenty-five Italian). The Italians should have prevailed, but instead, on September 11, at eleven o'clock in the morning, Campioni capitulated, thereby ending twenty-two years of Italy's partial, then full, sovereignty over the island of Rhodes.

And how was all of this, any of this, experienced in the Juderia?

"We felt two very different things," Stella tells me. "Especially later on, when we came to understand better what had happened, we felt shame, and anger, for the failure of the Italians—there were more of them; they had weapons, however imperfect; and they gave up after a very limited fight. In the moment, though, for the first few days we were absolutely terrified. We locked ourselves up in our homes as soon as curfew was called, around six o'clock when the shops were ordered closed. No one went out. Once, we heard the distinctive steps of a German soldier walking by—my mother said we should consider escaping by way of the terrace upstairs. He had come to the Juderia to sightsee, it turned out."

But then, curiously, nothing more happened—nothing more *seemed* to happen. The Germans, with their hands full, left the administration of the island to the Italian bureaucracy. Shops reopened. People went to the beach. In brief, life resumed, though it was a different, quieter, more subdued life. People no longer left their doors open all day long or called or sang to one another across the *kortijos*. In the evening, Miriam would be waiting at the door for the girls, anxious that they return home before the curfew. The noisy, boisterous, bustling Juderia was now muted and on uneasy alert.

49

When the news came that Campioni had ceded control of Rhodes to the Germans, Stella's friend Renzo Rossi was at lunch at the Benatars, a Jewish family who lived in the Marash. The Benatars' house was close to the carabinieri, thus close to the church of San Giovanni and the port. Rossi thanked his hosts for the meal, then told them he needed to go and rather abruptly for a man of such refined manners he got up from the table and walked out. Calmly but decisively he made his way past the church and down to the port, where a number of Greek sailors, having heard that the Germans had seized the island, were preparing to ferry people to Turkey on their sailboats. Rossi approached one, then another of them, removed all of the money from his wallet, and offered it in exchange for a place on one of these boats.

He wasn't the only Italian citizen to leave, or try to leave, that day. Menascé reports that from the top of Monte Smith Germans saw a large boat full of Italian officials tear off their uniforms and attempt to pass as ordinary citizens as they too tried to make it to Turkey; several young Jewish men were also on that first boat, which the Germans ordered sunk. Not everyone died. Some men swam back to Rhodes; others were picked up by a smaller boat that took them to Turkey.

Rossi succeeded in departing on a different vessel. He never returned to his villa, which the Germans soon requisitioned. He left behind his clothes, his books, his collection of antique coins. And Evangelina, who went on keeping house, for a while anyway.

The boat took him to Turkey, where the English counsel helped him to make it to Alexandria. From there he eventually went to Switzerland, where he had business connections, bank accounts, friends.

I ask Stella how such news arrived in the Juderia, whether it was printed in the paper, or came by word of mouth, or . . . ? The streets themselves spoke, she tells me. It was like when they learned that he was Jewish. No sooner had something happened, or been disclosed, than everyone knew.

After the war, Stella tried to find Rossi. In Florence she tracked down his sister, who told her that he had fallen gravely ill but was recovering in Switzerland. Eventually he wrote Stella a letter that caught up with her when she was in New York; he floated the idea of their arranging to meet again, but it was too late. "I told him I was not returning to Italy, not to live. Maybe not even to visit for a long time."

So what about Rossi, I ask Stella, going from the lunch table to the boat and into immediate exile? Did *that* not influence anyone's thinking?

"I suppose, I can't be sure now, that we all felt, Oh, this has something to do with business. He was Jewish, he had money, it was too risky for him to stay, too uncertain." She pauses. "Obviously now when I tell you that story—when I *hear* myself tell you that story—I hear it differently, but at the time we failed to see the consequences of the Germans taking over as clearly as he did."

And initially, at any rate, the Germans, Stella says, seemed utterly uninterested in the Jews. The curfew remained in effect, but it pertained to the island as a whole. The synagogues stayed open. They didn't issue any edicts that expanded the racial laws of 1938. They didn't compel them to wear stars. They didn't harass the residents of the Juderia. With the help of the Italian civil administration (which continued to govern the island; the Germans only assumed military control), these newest rulers over Rhodes were busy dispatching any Italian soldiers who had resisted them to prisoner-of-war camps and preparing, now that they had seized the island, for presumed Allied attacks. They had their hands full.

"This was our new reality, and we simply lived it. We had a lot on our minds that had nothing to do with our fate, like finding food, which was becoming scarce, and in my case worrying about my father's health. And anyway at the moment life in the Juderia went back to the way it had been—more or less."

50

Je suis juive.

Ça va.

Because Stella knew Kleemann's staff member, because the young women sang for all the men at the party (the second, later party) that evening, something quite astonishing—astonishing to me—happened after the Germans seized the island: Stella went, accompanied by a few friends, to see Kleemann himself, to ask him for a favor.

"You, a young Jewish woman, went to see Kleemann, the Nazi officer in command of Rhodes, to ask him for a favor?"

She answers with a placid nod.

"With your friends, who were also Jewish?"

Another nod.

"What made you think that was safe?"

"We didn't think if it was safe or if it wasn't safe. We simply went."

Stella and the Viennese fellow continued to run into each other at La Rotunda, she goes on to tell me, and she saw him again at the second party at the Sidises' where, joining in the singing that evening, was Stella S.'s older sister Vittoria, who had fallen in love with and married an Italian soldier, Ernesto Licitri (he was the owner of the radio the young women listened to at the first party). Like many of the Italian soldiers who remained on Rhodes after the Germans took control, Ernesto was about to be shipped off to a prisoner-of-war camp in Germany, and Vittoria was distraught. So Stella L. and her friends figured that, given that Stella L. had met Kleemann's staff member on the beach and had a few nice swims together, and that he had said *ça va* when she told him she was Jewish, and that he had asked them (on Kleemann's behalf) to sing *Tornerai*—and *J'attendrai*—they might as well try to go see Kleemann and ask if, for the sake of young love, the couple might stay together for a little while longer yet. What did they have to lose?

Stella L. and Stella S., Vittoria, and another Vittoria, Vittoria Cohen, who was a cousin of the Sidis sisters, walked across town to the Grand Master's palace, a formidable building put up by the Knights of St. John where the Germans had an office (for security reasons they established their main headquarters inland at Mount Profitis Ilias). Stella's acquaintance from the beach received and greeted them amicably and went to speak with Kleemann, who stepped outside of his office to listen to their request. He wrote down the name of the soldier, and then he went back to work. The meeting lasted three minutes—maybe.

The next day Ernesto was given a reprieve, for a few months at least. He would be given another one still before being sent off to Germany in April 1944. His wife, having converted to Catholicism in order to be married in the Church, would be spared from the deportation.

<h1 style="text-align:center">51</h1>

During the war years the young women of the Juderia grew up much faster than they would have otherwise and assumed responsibilities that previously would have fallen to the sons in the family. With the sons, most of them, abroad, seeking or making their fortunes, the daughters didn't exactly become their brothers but started living with a freedom and independence that would have been unimaginable ten years earlier and might never have been granted—or assumed by—them if more men had been on the scene.

These young women were fluid, adaptable, and brave. Unlike their parents, they spoke Italian, which made it easy for them to bridge the world of the Juderia and the world of greater Rhodes. And they rose to the challenges that came at them. Renée and Stella were quick to realize that they had to take care of their parents. In order to help feed the family, Stella became acquainted, and nimbly, with the ways of the black market. Renée had been the first to go to work, in the office of the lawyer San

Pietro; now Stella also followed, taking a job in one of Renzo Rossi's offices that he had arranged for her and that she was able to hold on to even after he left. She did basic accounting at a long wooden table in a room full of books. Her immediate supervisor understood that she would never have had this job if she hadn't been Rossi's friend and regarded her "*di malocchio*"—suspiciously—but Stella didn't care. The family needed her income. And besides, Renée worked upstairs in the very same building, another one that had been built by the Knights, as did Stella Sidis and San Pietro's daughters, Cristina and Bice, all of them at an import-export firm, the Commerciale. At lunch the young women would meet outside on the large stone staircase that connected the lower to the upper floors of the building. They hung out with their friends Despola, Mihali, and Yoti Papathanasis, who worked in the same building. The ever more reduced Rhodeslis embraced their Greek peers; everyone was determined to have a good time, no matter what.

The diminishment of Yehuda, the paterfamilias, haunts the story of the Levis' final months in Rhodes. It started back in 1938 when under the racial laws he lost control of his business, and it was compounded by Victor's departure and Yehuda's own advancing blindness. By the time of the German occupation, Yehuda had stopped working entirely, and the family was living off what the girls brought in and their savings, which he kept in a locked drawer at home.

"I remember the constant worry about the money running out," Stella says. "I remember my father having to feel for the cash in the drawer, because he could no longer see."

Work and religious practice had been the anchors of Yehuda's life. Now that one was completely taken away from him, how did that feel? Stella has told me before that, like most couples, Yehuda and Miriam never went out together; she adds that she never saw him hold a child's hand, or play with his or anyone else's children, or wander outside, as her mother did, to listen to Nisso Cohen's Greek friends who came to play music in the neighborhood at the end of Shabbat. Certainly he never went out for *passeggiate* along the Mandrakio, as Miriam did, or to the cinema or to swim at the beach.

Formerly Yehuda had worked so hard that he rarely came home for lunch—there was always an argument about who would deliver his midday meal, in its three-part stacking metal lunch box, a task that more often fell to Stella since Renée was embarrassed to have a father who was too industrious to come home to eat. Yehuda had raised, and married or sent off, five of his seven children. He had employed his brother-in-law, Isaac Notrica, in his business for as long as it was viable (Isaac left the island in 1940, taking Felicie with him), and he paid for the passage to America, as Stella has mentioned, of his nephews Joe and Eliakim Hasson, a gesture that was repeated across many families in the Juderia: a cousin who had money helped one who did not; a different one might repay, setting in motion a circle of generosity. Now this, all of this, the working, the providing, the helping, the facilitating, the managing, had come to an end. "Imagine what it felt like when you could no longer do your part," Stella tells me, "when you could no longer do any of what you used to."

In late 1943 and early 1944 the family's savings did actually begin to run out, and it became Miriam's turn to pitch in the only way she could: by pawning her jewelry to yet another cousin of hers, a certain Behor Pihas, beginning with the big *manillas de chatón*—gold bracelets that matched ones that had been sent to America with Selma and Sara—and soon continuing with the pearl necklaces, the gold earrings, the stack of thinner gold bracelets that was the custom for the women of the Juderia to pile up on one arm nearly as far as their elbows. All these pieces went to this cousin the pawnbroker who, having Turkish citizenship, managed to escape the deportation.

After the war, Behor Pihas still had Miriam's jewelry in his possession, but when he reached out to Stella's brothers, they couldn't agree on how much money to pay to redeem it, so they let everything go.

"By then," Stella says, "I was beyond caring about such things myself. Way beyond."

52

Stella opens the door looking as though she hadn't slept the night before, or very little. Her eyes are glassy and distant, and smudged with shadows. She drops heavily into her customary armchair.

"I saw two of my sisters in a dream last night, Sara and Renée," she says. "*C'era tutto un pasticcio*—I told you before Renée did not care for that kind of word, didn't I? In the dream they were confused about our house in Rhodes, about who owned it now . . ."

"Who does own it, Stella? Do you know?"

"When I went back, finally, in the seventies, the late seventies, I was able to ask what had happened after we were deported. I learned that the Greeks on the island were all starving, they broke in and ate everything, took everything they could sell, in the winter they burned our furniture for firewood. I don't even know if this is true . . ."

And the house? "It belonged to my grandmother, remember, and there was a disagreement with some cousins of mine, who believed they owned a part of it. It was like my mother's jewelry—we let it go. We sold our share for very little, we basically gave up this last of our tangible connections to the Juderia. No one in my family wanted the house. Not a single member of the community, you realize, went back to live in Rhodes full time. Many of us didn't even go back to visit for years, decades . . ."

In the dream first Renée, then Sara appeared, and there was this *pasticcio*, this confusion, about a house. At first it seemed to be the house in Rhodes, and then it became a different house, a modern house, and in the dream Renée said to Stella, "Don't you want to come to *this* house? *This* house is better than all the others."

Dislocation, relocation, a confusion about where home was, *what* home was: it's hard to imagine a more fitting dream for Stella to have, especially now, given the topic of our recent conversations.

She goes on to tell me that dreams have played an important role in her life. And not only her dreams either. Renée once had a dream, she says, that she never told anyone about before, except for their mother at the time, and Stella, and Stella has never told it to anyone before either.

First she sets the scene: two doors off the Kay Ancha, next to the Dante Alighieri, there was a building with a balcony that overlooked the square. In Renée's dream, two older women were standing on this balcony. One was their grandmother Sara Notrica, and the other Sara's sister Mazaltov de Yakov Pasha who had (in waking life) left Rhodes and gone to live in Seattle. Several other women, also older, were there too, on the balcony, but Renée couldn't remember who they were. Below, down at the level of the street, two rabbis were standing, and the entire community was passing before them. The rabbis were saying, "You go here" and "You go there." Among the passers-by were Stella, Sara (Sara Notrica, Stella's cousin), and Renée, both of whom ended up at Auschwitz with her. Sara Notrica the grandmother (who was also grandmother to Sara Notrica, Stella and René's cousin) cried out, "But these are my *grandchildren!*"

When Renée recounted this dream to their mother the following morning, Miriam ran and lit an oil lamp at the synagogue, saying as she flew out the door, "*Todo bueno se va a ser*"—everything will be all right.

Renée dreamed this scene before—how long before?—the deportation. Months. Several months.

"Renée wasn't at all like this, though," Stella says. "She wasn't particularly mystical. She herself couldn't believe she had this dream. She kept shaking her head, I kept shaking my head . . ."

There was something about the Juderia, Stella goes on to tell me. People had dreams and visions, they saw apparitions—her uncle Isaac Notrica, before he left for America, was on his way to say selichot in the early hours of the morning before the High Holy Days when not far from the Puerta de la Mar, where he lived, he saw a group of men, giants, three times an average man's height, walking in a slow procession along the road. When he told Miriam about them afterward he described them as *los buenos de mosotros* (*m* sometimes replacing *n* in their Judeo-Spanish)—the best of us. That is to say: angels, or men as angels. He knew what he had seen; he knew who they were.

Stella had a significant dream of her own after the Germans had occupied the island and were beginning to send the Italian soldiers and officers to prisoner-of-war camps. Luigi Noferini had returned to Italy for the summer—the summer of 1943. He'd joined up with the partisans and never came back to Rhodes, because it became impossible after that point. He left behind his great friend Gennaro Tescione.

"Gennaro and I spent a lot of time together, we went out, we sang, we confided in each other, we exchanged poems . . . he *was* a poem, he wrote poems too, some of them to me. I have a whole notebook of his writing. One day maybe I will show it to you . . ."

Stella here retreats into one of her silences.

"I've told you about him before. But I've never told you this."

Her dream: she had it in December 1943, on the night of the eighth to be precise. Tescione is naked, lying spread out in the piazza that is the center of the Juderia. Just that: an image, a silent image of this naked man she cared for so deeply, Gennaro Tescione.

Stella woke up anxious and, like Renée before her, ran to describe the dream to her mother, who said at once, "Go to the mezuzah and say a prayer, then run to the synagogue and say another prayer . . . *hurry.*"

Stella did as she was told, but the prayers didn't help. The whole day she remained unsettled. Finally she took her bicycle and went to the Albergo delle Rose, where she knew that the officials on the island ate in a certain room at a certain time. Just before she reached the Piazza d'Italia she was intercepted by Tescione's *soldato attendente*, who said, "Signorina Stella, I was just coming to look for you. The order came that Tescione has to leave the island and is to be sent to prison in Germany. The Germans told him that he had to present himself and he has gone home to prepare."

"To prepare?" asked Stella.

"To pack his clothes, his things."

An hour later, a different friend of Tescione's, a lieutenant by the name of Nino Garzolini, came to the door to tell her that Tescione was in the hospital. Rather than agreeing to be taken to prison, he had shot himself. Later that night he died.

How was it possible, I ask Stella, that she had seen this, a version of this, in her dream?

"Life was like that in the Juderia. We felt things, rumblings, forecasts. The unseen was more . . . accessible to us, I suppose, maybe because we were such a close community, or maybe . . . I don't know why, really. Such a thing would never happen here. I scarcely know a single person in this building, let alone here in the Village, and I've lived in the neighborhood for more than half a century."

Because it was a suicide they would not allow a funeral to be held in the big church, San Giovanni; instead it was in a smaller church, San Francesco. "We all went, even my mother with a friend of hers; they stayed outside, but Renée and I and Sara Notrica and Vittoria Cohen and several other of my friends, we went in . . ." She pauses. "Never in my life . . . never have I felt . . ."

Stella runs out of words, but her face communicates for her. More than seventy-five years later it's clear how haunted and troubled she is by this death.

Tescione had left letters behind. To his colonel he wrote, in formal, dignified language, that it was clear to him that he and the other soldiers could not, at the moment, avenge the insult that was perpetrated against Italy in the Aegean and that he refused to be taken prisoner after a surrender *"senza onore"*—without honor. He said that he had come to a decision that felt compulsory to him:

> As a longtime officer in the Aegean, whose ethics are old-school, I will remain here, buried with a bullet in my forehead that I am calmly placing there myself.
>
> In deciding to offer myself up in this way I've prepared myself in my soul, and I proceed with strength, serenity, faith, and an inner peace that I've possibly never before experienced . . .
>
> Greet Italy for me, when she is risen again.
>
> And tell her that I loved her more than my own life.

To his father he wrote:

> People will tell you that I was a worthy soldier. As such I did
> my best to honor the name of our family.
>
> I embrace you, mother, everyone. I feel closer to you than
> ever before.

When they returned to the Juderia, one of the girls in the neighborhood whispered, "Look at Stella, shedding tears for her *fidanzato italiano.*"

Stella shakes her head. "Who wouldn't shed tears at the loss of a human being like that?"

53

And then, in the spring of 1944, the British began bombing the island in an attempt to take it back from the Germans, and the entire atmosphere changed again.

As long as the British were targeting the airfield out near Maritsa, the old city was safe. But when they switched to the German supply ships anchored in the harbor, and the raids happened during daylight rather than after dark, the situation felt much more dire. The harbor was near to the Juderia, and the bombers often missed their targets.

Each time an airplane flew overhead, or the air-raid siren went off, Miriam turned pale—worse, yellow—and trembled uncontrollably, while Yehuda remained calm. "If it comes, it comes," he said. "If I die, I die." More than once, even before the siren sounded, Stella found her mother already in the shelter, hiding in the corner with a coat on, terrified. The shelter wasn't underground but on the ground floor in a room under the Turiels' that had a vaulted ceiling and had been reinforced with sandbags. When they heard a siren in the middle of the night, they would hurry down in their pajamas; they'd wait until the all-clear bell sounded, and then they'd return to bed.

Miriam thought Stella was crazy to insist on going upstairs to help Amelie Leon, a neighbor with a broken foot, make it all the way downstairs only to have to hobble all the way back up again. (Amelie was the sister of Rebecca Leon, the young Zionist who had gone to Palestine with the passengers of the *Rim*.) But Stella couldn't have lived with herself if she'd left Amelie alone and something happened to her; no.

Then on February 8, 1944, an errant British bomb killed eight people in the Juderia, among them two children, who were incinerated. Because they vanished into thin air, at first rumors circulated that they had been kidnapped, taken as mascots. "It wasn't true," Stella says. "I knew the family, I knew the house. The whole thing just imploded. Not a trace was left behind." Either the Italians or the Germans (more likely the Italians) cleaned up the rubble quickly, adding to the feeling that this family had disappeared.

After the February bombing nobody wanted to sleep above the ground floor. People stopped sleeping, period. Everyone was jittery, preoccupied, afraid.

Something now shifted in Stella too: "I no longer recognized the Juderia. It wasn't simply the physical aspect of the neighborhood, but my feelings about it." Now, when Stella came home to the familiar streets, they weren't the same to her. Her own little piece of the earth had become other. She had begun to detach herself from it. "The Juderia was foreign to me, I almost didn't recognize it. This was something I could never have imagined happening, not ever."

In April 1944, on the first day of Passover, Stella, Renée, and Sara Notrica agreed to meet for a visit in the bright sunshine on the staircase of the building that housed their offices. They had distributed themselves, as usual, on different steps and were deep in conversation when around ten in the morning British aircraft flew overhead. A few minutes later the siren sounded, in reverse order to the norm. They saw the bombs fall out of the sky, dark lozenges dropping menacingly toward the Juderia. In unison they stood up and began to run. When they reached the neighborhood they saw destruction, rubble everywhere. Stella hurried to find her parents, who were in the shelter. Miriam was violently shaking, but she was alive.

Others were not: twenty-six people were killed that morning as they left the synagogue.

"How do we stay here?" Miriam asked.

"We don't," Stella answered.

They packed up a few necessary things and went to stay outside of the Juderia with Stella Sidis and her family, where they spread mattresses on the floor and hunkered down for a few days. Then their Greek friends the Papathanasises found them a house to rent in Trianda, a nearby village, and took them to live there. Within days they were joined by other families from the Juderia.

After they moved out to Trianda, Stella and Renée returned to the Juderia only once, to collect clothes and supplies.

The neighborhood was quiet, empty, not quite abandoned, but slumbering, as if a spell had been cast over it. The Levi sisters made their way through the streets without speaking or looking at each other. "I knew that the life that had been lived there, with such intensity and for so many years—centuries—was finished," Stella says. "Even if on that actual day I couldn't put this into words, it was what I knew, what I sensed, in my heart, in my flesh . . ."

They packed a few bags, collected whatever food they could carry, then closed and locked the front door to the house they'd lived in for all of their conscious lives. They left everything intact: their remaining clothes, their linens, furniture, photos, and memorabilia, all of it.

"As soon as the war is over," Renée said to Stella, "we'll be back."

54

"So it was July, and you were in Trianda," I say, wondering if Stella will tell me in detail what comes next. She has threatened not to, and upon more than one occasion, but after all our weeks, our months, and now years of talking, she surprises me. She simply picks up the story:

"So it was July. The nineteenth of July, 1944, and the men were told to present themselves first, with their documents, at the *aeronautica*." The *aeronautica* was the former headquarters of the Italian air force in viale Regina Elena; now it was occupied by the German *kommandantur*.

The order came from a German officer, who went to see Jacob Franco, the president of the community, and explained that all Jewish men age thirteen and above were to assemble there the next day.

"I heard this," Stella continues, "and I told myself, my father he is almost blind, he cannot possibly go. I'll go in his place."

Stella took her father's identity card and appeared at the *aeronautica* with the men. She approached the German officer in charge, someone she had never seen before; he pointed her in the direction of a man who spoke Judeo-Spanish.

At the time Stella didn't think it was odd to hear someone translating from German into Judeo-Spanish. She was grateful, in this context, merely to hear it spoken—with perfect fluency, as it happened, by a man who, Stella learned some years later, turned out to be Pepo (or Costa) Recanati (or Ricanati, or Rekanatis; the spelling bounces around), who had been conscripted to work for the Germans, on whose behalf, first at Salonika and now at Rhodes, he was tasked with putting agitated, frightened Jews at ease. (He also worked for himself, negotiating bribes, apparently with tacit German permission, to help the occasional member of the community who fell through a lucky bureaucratic crack escape arrest.)

Recanati sent Stella outside with other worried women who had also come to the *aeronautica*. She was joined by her friends Mihali and Yoti

Papathanasis, who had come to try to understand what was going on and what they might do to help their friends. After a while Recanati announced that the women were to come the following day, with any of their missing husbands, and their children, and clothes, and all of their valuables, meaning jewelry and money, and some food. If they did not appear as instructed, they were told, the men would be shot.

Back in Trianda Mihali and Yoti offered to marry Stella and Renée, with the idea being that if they married in church and converted, they would be safe. The sisters were touched but could not conceive of leaving their parents to fend for themselves.

The Germans, meanwhile, went into the villages and, with the help of some Jewish "volunteers," spread the word and searched for any Jews who might not have heard these directives.

"We still—*still*—had no idea why they were collecting us," Stella says. "We thought they were taking us to a camp, maybe another island, to work. And that we would need money to pay for our food. It's amazing how the human mind tries to make sense out of—" She pauses. "Anyway we did as were told. We went home, and we packed our bags."

The next morning, when Stella appeared with her mother and sister at the *aeronautica*, she was wearing a summer dress, white with green polka dots, and a favorite pair of *sahariane*, sandals that were much in fashion in Rhodes and had white leather straps and cork soles, a classic summer look of the time.

Miriam wore a light dress and a jacket and had sewn money and jewelry into her belt.

Some of the women followed orders and handed their jewels over immediately, but not Miriam, and not Signora Benveniste, the proprietor of the finest jewelry shop in town. Signora Benveniste flushed her valuables down the toilet, which promptly overflowed. Then she began to wail. "The poor thing," Stella says, shaking her head. "She went mad."

One by one the Jewish men and women, united now, were asked for their names, which were crossed off a list. Then they were locked into the *aeronautica* for two days and two nights—July 21 and July 22. They slept on the floor and ate what food they'd brought with them. The bathrooms overflowed. Water ran out.

Kleemann was nowhere to be seen. Instead these new German officers appeared to be in control. They were SS, recently arrived from Athens and the first ever seen on the island.

On the morning of July 23, which was deliberately a Sunday, as Stella told me when I visited her in Rhodes in 2015, the Germans sounded the air raid sirens, though there were no air raids. The sirens sounded, and all but one member of the community—largely old people, women, and children, approximately 1,650 of them—lined up. With Jacob Franco at their head, they were ordered to keep their eyes on the ground as they were escorted through town by the German military police, a small unit from the German infantry, and a handful of carabinieri. They proceeded toward the Mandrakio, then along the ancient walls of the city toward the port. Babies and toddlers had to be carried. Some of the old were on crutches. Children held on to their parents, parents their children.

As Stella describes this day to me, I recall a refrain from one of her stories about her childhood in the Juderia, that phrase, called out and echoing over the cobbled streets: *Pasa la misva, pasa la misva*—only in her childhood, the cortege was for just one man, or woman, and Stella and her family were safely at home, with the doors doubly locked and the windows shut, hiding from death and hiding from grief. This instead was a cortege made up of—and for—the entire community, 90 percent of whom were heading to their own deaths, although they had no idea at the time.

55

Stella, unsurprisingly, did not follow the instructions to the letter. She looked up; surreptitiously she looked around. No one was there. No one watched. No one protested.

She knew, by sight, one of the carabinieri who was helping to monitor their procession. He followed along on a motorcycle. Years later she would see him in Naples, at the port. He recognized her—they recognized each other—but out of fear, or shame, he turned away, then vanished into the crowd.

At one point as she was walking Stella found herself staring at a section of the thick, solid city wall put up by the Knights into which a small window had been cut, likely during the Turkish period. On the other side of this wall lived several Notricas, including Stella's Tia Rachel. It was in the courtyard that backed up against it, at the marriage of Tia Rachel's daughter Lea Amato to Salomone Hugno, that Stella first saw Luigi Noferini dance, and danced with him. The window itself was reached by way of a wooden staircase that led up to a tiny room with no apparent purpose. Stella associated this room with her great-aunt Lea Galante Notrica, who suffered from asthma. She was in the habit of climbing (slowly, carefully) the wooden staircase that gave access to the room with no purpose, where she found, in fact, a very particular purpose: without having to leave the neighborhood, she was able to lean out of the window the Turks had pierced into the walls the Knights had built and breathe the sea air.

Lea Notrica was the sister of Avram Galante, the writer and educator who had been instrumental in bringing the Alliance Israélite Universelle to Rhodes, which began the slow process of westernizing this old, stable, storied community of human beings who were, at that moment, being led by this very window on their way to being deported from the island. The window was the last thing Stella saw that connected her to the Juderia.

It took several hours for all 1,650 people to reach the port, where three dilapidated cargo boats were anchored and waiting. The old went down into the hold, where they were wedged together. Stella's one thought was for her father, that he would make it safely aboard, and be able to sit down with enough space to stretch out his legs. Once she and Renée saw to their parents, and their cousin Sara Notrica saw to hers,

they joined the other young people up on deck, to be in the air, and to be able to see the sea.

Finally the boat pulled up anchor and glided out of the port and then into open water.

Stella had never before seen the island from this perspective, or this distance. She stood there steadily watching until it became smaller and smaller. Eventually it turned into a spot, then a speck. And then, just like that, it disappeared over the horizon.

56

How did it happen that in a matter of days a handful of German SS officers were able to find, identify, round up, and ship off 1,650 human beings who lived on the island of Rhodes, territory that had come under their control only ten months earlier?

The short answer is that the Germans mounted many efficient deportations, but in this case they had help from the Italians. Specifically, from the Italian carabinieri on the island.

Stella, her fellow survivors, and scholars who have written about the Jewish community of Rhodes all suspected that the Italians had a role in the deportation, but no one knew what that role was, exactly, until Eirini Toliou and Marco Clementi found evidence that the Italians had prepared a list of the Jews of Rhodes and had handed that list over to the Germans.

As Michele Sarfatti, Simon Levis Sullam, Michael Livingston, and other writers on the Fascist period have pointed out, the deportations in Italy were often carried out with the complicit, or explicit, participation of the Italian police, even in certain cases with the participation of ordinary Italians; but until the archive on Rhodes was examined and reported on by Clementi and Toliou in their book *Gli ultimi ebrei di Rodi*, no one knew to what degree, and in what way, the Italians appeared to contribute to this particular, and particularly heartbreaking, deportation.

To read Clementi and Toliou's book is to peer behind Stella's memories of the deportation to see one take on the ugly underpinnings, the roots and tentacles, that made July 23 possible. As the historian Anthony McElligott points out in a stringent observation in his contribution to *The Holocaust in Greece*, "Survivors cannot be expected to know in intricate detail what was happening to them; they were not privy to plans to kill them." Like the informant's letter, but far more significant, Clementi and Toliou's discoveries reveal the counter story; all that was hidden from Stella as she was living this experience now sharpens into troubling view.

In their almost forensic approach to the documents they found, Clementi and Toliou establish "beyond a doubt"—their phrase—that at the request of police headquarters, the office of vital records compiled a list of all the Jews residing in Rhodes and delivered it to the Germans around the time that Anton Burger, the former commandant of the ghetto at Theresienstadt/Terezín and an associate of Adolf Eichmann, was put in charge of the Aegean. On the night of July 12 to 13 Burger paid a surprise visit to Kleemann. Despite some conflict regarding the chain of command between Kleemann and Burger ("an antisemitic thug," per McElligott, "who could be counted on to ride roughshod over any opposition"), the fact remained that the deportation was issued in Heinrich Himmler's name and, in the end, went ahead as ordered.

The Germans were in charge, incontrovertibly, but Clementi and Toliou have found documents attesting to the fact that as early as April— so, well before Burger's visit—the carabinieri had asked the municipal administration for a list of Jews on the island. Clementi and Toliou do their best to identify the hands these documents passed through and that annotated them; they investigate the pencil marks, the file folders, the official stamps, the (minor) contradictions, the look, the smell, the very *weight* of this material, until you can almost feel them pausing to catch their breath before they remark, "Sometimes complicated explanations seem simple, even banal."

They go on to say that

> the deportation and consequential destruction of the
> Jews of Rhodes took place only because the Italian au-

thorities fully collaborated in its implementation . . .
It's not just a matter of assembling the 1944 list of the
Rhodian Jews to deport, it's the great diligence with
which the Italians participated beforehand, during, and
afterward.

It would be tidy to be able to leave the story here, but Luca Pignataro, a historian who has looked at these and other related documents,
sees the Italians as far less culpable: late in his book on the Italian Dodecanese he draws attention to Italian authorities who, in fact, protested
the deportation. Somehow it's not surprising to learn that it might take
time to come to a conclusive reading of what actually transpired between
the Italian and German authorities in the period leading up to July 23,
1944—if one can, in fact, ever be reached. But the facts remain: the Germans had the names; the names led to the people; and the people were
taken away.

Stella, when I discuss all this with her, takes the wider perspective: "It
just makes no sense," she says, "none of it." Even after all these years,
she adds, she still cannot grasp why the Germans, who by July 1944 had
already lost all of Italy south of and including Rome and were about to
withdraw from Florence, spent so much effort, energy, and money to
round up these innocent people, most of them very old or very young,
and ship them all the way to Auschwitz to be murdered: "What on earth
was the purpose?"

57

From Stella's point of view, Rhodes disappeared off the horizon.
From the point of view of those left behind on the island, the boats did
the same.

About fifty Jews remained.

One was an old woman of ninety who lived alone and whom no one had told about the arrest or the deportation. A Greek family found her wandering around the ghostly Juderia. She was starving and disoriented. A month later, she died.

Lina Amato, the eight-year-old daughter of Alberto Amato and Renata Cori, had been hidden, effectively adopted by Bianca and Gerolamo Sotgiu, the literature professor who was one of the teachers in the "secret" school. The adoption saved her life.

Vittoria Sidis, now Licitri, had married that Italian soldier, Ernesto Licitri, whom Stella and her friends had tried to help out by appealing to Kleemann. Because she had converted to Catholicism, her name was no longer on the list of the Jews.

And Selahattin Ülkümen, the Turkish consul on the island, who had only arrived in the summer of 1943 and was in his early thirties, managed to rescue forty-three Jews. These people were former Ottoman subjects (or married to, or the children of) who had either lost their Italian citizenship because of the racial laws or never acquired it and thus had become Turkish, he maintained, by default.

Some of these people came to him; some were brought to his attention after they bribed Costa Recanati; some—like Stella's neighbors the Turiels, whose mother, Matilde, had been born in İzmir in 1910—the counsel found and plucked out of the line as they were on their way into the *aeronautica*. Ülkümen insisted that, as Turkey was still neutral and did not allow discrimination on the basis of religion, it would create a major diplomatic incident if these people were to be deported from the island. Although he was helped by the fact that the rule-following Germans were disinclined to deport citizens of still-neutral countries, he nevertheless displayed considerable diplomatic grit in helping to save the lives that he did.

These Turkish Jews who remained behind did not have an easy time of it, unsurprisingly. The Germans required that they present themselves each morning at the *kommandantur*; by the end of the year, and into early 1945, they had all chosen or had been pressured to emigrate to

Turkey. The day the last Turkish Jew left the island, Rhodes was effectively rendered *judenrein.*

58

The journey from Rhodes to Piraeus lasted eight days, including stops. The conditions were deplorable: Human waste accumulated below decks, where the old people were crowded together. Food dwindled. Everyone was desperately thirsty. The sun was intense, the anxiety thick.

Stella found a way to ask the (German) captain for a lemon, as her mother was feeling faint; remarkably he arranged for one to be given to her.

He had, she says, a face that made her feel she could trust him. He didn't seem very happy to be doing this job, steering this boat. Or so she imagined, or decided.

Her worry for her parents, like so many of the young people for their older parents, was constant. Yehuda and Miriam sat quietly, with grave, confused expressions on their faces. Now and then they recited or sang prayers. They didn't ask questions—not that Stella or anyone else had any answers. It was difficult to know what they were thinking, Stella tells me, though at that point they still appeared to believe, as most of the passengers seemed to, that they were being taken to a different island to live for a time. Which island and for what length of time? No one had any idea.

At Leros another vessel joined theirs; it was carrying approximately a hundred Jews from the island of Kos, all of the local Jewish community except for thirteen people who had been saved, again, by Ülkümen, yet again because they were Turkish citizens.

The boats from Rhodes had docked in Leros in order to pick up the following: food, water, and the island's one Jew.

Near Samos, Stella again asked the captain for a favor. She had not bathed for days, and it was scorching on the deck. She wondered if it was possible to take a swim, she and her friend Clara Gabriel—"We were the two great swimmers"—and the captain, surprisingly, gave her permission. The two young women took off their dresses and dove into the deep blue water in their underclothes. Afterward a rope ladder was lowered down so that they could climb back on board.

A boy had wanted to join them, but he was not allowed. Stella wonders whether the captain thought he was so strong that he might swim to shore, and therefore escape.

Along the way five people died. Their bodies were thrown unceremoniously overboard.

In hindsight Stella has other, sharper thoughts to offer about this journey. Not thoughts; questions without answers.

"Why didn't we rebel? There were hundreds of us and only a few of them. Why didn't we, why didn't *I*, think of taking some kind of action?" (Was it because, I wonder privately, she'd been given that lemon and allowed that swim?)

And—

"We passed by all kinds of Turkish ships. Why didn't they do anything?"

And—

"The English were in these waters too. They had a blockade around Rhodes. Surely they knew what was going on? How hard—I should say, how *easy*—would it have been for them to stop these boats? I blame the Allies as much as the Germans. Why didn't they do anything? Because they didn't want to risk their boats or their troops for a handful of Jews?"

59

When after eight days they arrived at the Athenian port of Piraeus, uniformed men Stella had never seen before—Gestapo—were waiting with trucks to transport them to the prison at Haidari, where they would be held for three more days before being transferred to the trains that would take them to Auschwitz.

"After eight days on those boats, the old could barely walk," Stella tells me. "My father couldn't stand up on his own. He was with my uncle Mazliah, who was helping him. One of the Germans was about to hit my father when I hurried over and took the blow for him. I didn't understand anything. There was so much I didn't understand."

At Haidari the men and women were separated and made to undress completely, to see if they were hiding any jewels. Anything they found was immediately confiscated, the jewels Miriam had sewn into her belt included.

Once again Stella, almost without thinking about what she was doing, sought to bend the rules. She approached a guard and, through a Greek man who helped to interpret, asked for permission to check on her father; she couldn't bear not knowing how he was doing. At the men's barracks she found her uncle Mazliah and asked him what they needed, and he answered water. Stella discovered that someone had hooked a hose up to a fountain, and that everyone was running toward it, so she did the same and managed to bring water to her father and her uncle.

Thinking ahead, she'd brought a bowl with her. Already she understood how important it was to be prepared.

Other people weren't so lucky. One man, Esther Fintz Menascé reports, complained so much of thirst that he was given urine to drink; he died that afternoon. He was one of several people to die of dehydration.

Menascé's own grandfather Michael, a deeply religious man, objected to undressing in order to be searched, which so infuriated the German guards that they beat him to death.

At Haidari their ranks grew when they were joined by somewhere between seven hundred and nine hundred Jews from near Athens. On August 3, 1944, these Jews and the Jews from Rhodes and Kos, and the one

Jew from Leros, were loaded onto trucks and taken to the train station, where they were transferred to freight cars.

Virtually at the last moment, the Turkish consul, likely alerted by Selahattin Ülkümen, managed to save a further handful of people who had Turkish citizenship. Among them was Alberto Franco, son of the president of the community, whose wife was Turkish.

Everyone else was crammed into the train and began the long grueling journey north.

60

"You know how we often speak about my memory?" Stella says. "Well, now we come to a period where there are blank spots. I've lost much of the time on the train. Try as I do, other than my family, I cannot see the faces of the people, nearly seventy in all, who were locked up with us in that car. I expect that's because it was so unbearable."

It was unbearable, but Stella had no choice other than to bear it. In fact, when the doors opened, she already had a plan. She hurried onto the train, carrying her parents' bags in order to stake out a place for them next to a high window. She had noticed the window from the outside (it was one of only two in the car) and had plotted her movements beforehand.

She planted herself there and waited for Renée and her parents to join her. Miriam and Yehuda sat on their bags and were able to breathe. The window, which seemed at first a small thing, turned out to be critical because of the intense heat and the quality of the air in the car, which became more and more toxic the longer they traveled.

When Stella mentions the bags, I can't help but think of the suitcase she had packed when she was fourteen, the one that was to accompany her to university in Italy. When I say this to her she nods, then points out that, as fate would have it, the first time she ever traveled away from Rhodes, she traveled to Auschwitz—not that she or any of them knew where they were going when they boarded the train. And again she reminds me that, until they arrived there, they had never in their lives heard the word *Auschwitz* said, not once.

Gradually her parents began to understand *some*thing. Her father used the word *exodus*. Her mother asked questions: "Are we leaving Greece? Are we in Yugoslavia?" Stella, with access to the window, answered as best as she could. Her best was not definitive.

The train passed through Greece and Yugoslavia, yes, then Hungary and Czechoslovakia before reaching its destination in Poland. The journey lasted thirteen days.

People relieved themselves in a bucket. For Yehuda and Miriam, Stella and Renée rigged a kind of curtain, so that they could at least have those few moments of privacy.

The girls stood much of the time. Now and then Stella would sit on her mother's knees and try to sleep for a few moments, even though she knew that she was likely causing Miriam pain.

At one point the train stopped at a station, and through that high window Stella saw an Italian soldier, one of five or six who had accompanied them, patrolling the platform to make sure no one escaped. She engaged him in conversation, asking him where they were, and how much longer he thought the journey would take, and so on. After the train started up again, he brought her some bread. He did this not once, but three times.

Finally she asked him, "Where are they taking us, do you know?" and he shook his head. "They make us get off before the last stop, Signorina."

Stella's great-uncle Yehuda Notrica, the one who traveled so often to the Holy Land that he earned the nickname "Haji," died halfway through the journey. When the train stopped at a station somewhere in Czechoslovakia, his body was taken off, along with the bodies of other people (more than twenty in all, by the end of the journey) who had died.

"Where did they bury him?" I ask Stella.

"What ditch did they dump him in, you mean."

Stella's Tia Rachel, who lived behind Haji Yehuda and helped look after his wife, Lea, followed his body out of the train to grieve for him. She began wailing, right there in the train station, a final postscript to *los lloros* enacted far away from Rhodes, and with no one there to stop her now.

At this station, where the dead bodies, including her great-uncle's, were being unloaded, Stella noticed a pump, the kind with a lever that you had to operate in order to bring up water. Using mime and gestures, she approached the officer in charge, German this time, and asked if she might avail herself of the water to wash her hair. And he said yes. Like the captain on the ship who gave her a lemon and allowed her to swim, like the soldier and the bread, he permitted her (or mollified her with) this one human comfort.

Stella called out to her cousin Sara Notrica, who was in the next car, and within seconds she appeared by Stella's side. "I grabbed a bar of soap from my bag, and Renée and Sara and I went down together. Of course, my mother began to tremble, she turned white, she thought we'd never come back. But I had my eye on that water, and I went straight for it. We took turns pumping and washing, washing and pumping. I washed my hair and Renée and Sara washed theirs. And my face. I washed my face and they washed their faces."

While they were on the platform Stella noticed the stationmaster's children staring at them. From the look in their eyes she understood how awful they must have appeared, before they washed. Maybe even after.

61

On August 16, 1944, three and a half weeks after the boats sailed from Rhodes, the deportees arrived at Auschwitz.

At some point during the night before, the train stopped and, just as he had told Stella he would, the Italian soldier and his comrades stepped off.

The sun was coming up as they pulled into the station. When the doors opened, prisoners from Salonika stepped into the cars to help with the suitcases. Speaking in Judeo-Spanish, they whispered, "Give the babies to the old people." "But why," Stella asked one of them, "when the old people are so tired?"

No one answered, because SS guards stood outside within earshot. Only afterward did Stella understand that these men from Salonika were trying to save the mothers who, if they were holding a child, would be consigned to an all but certain death. Without a child, providing they looked healthy, there was a chance they might live. The SS guards waited behind because of the fleas, the stench, and the filth. Right away they started separating the men from the women. Stella's father could only see from one eye, so she said to her uncle Mazliah, "Take Papa by the hand." Her uncle said, "Don't worry."

Men in uniforms decided who was fit, who was not. Stella, by instinct, stood by her mother; she and Renée flanked Miriam and covered their heads with scarves so that the three of them looked similar. Dogs circled. The scarves didn't fool anyone. With the gesture of a hand—one officer, one hand—Stella understood that she had to let her mother go. Miriam, Miriam's sister Tia Rachel, and Rachel's daughter, Lea, who was holding her son Pippo, a particular favorite of Stella's, all stepped aside. "We'll see you soon," they said.

Even after their experience of the train they continued to believe they would all be in the camps together, living separately from the old, maybe, or maybe given the task of taking care of them, cooking for them, and so on; or possibly they would be working and the old would stay "home" and clean the barracks and do the cooking. "It was a fantastical story we told ourselves, a notion or a rumor we embroidered into reassurance; we were still thinking like we were in Rhodes, thinking everything would work out. It was naïveté masquerading as hope, or the other way around."

62

Stella, Renée, their cousin Sara, and the other young women were sent into a large room, where they were instructed to take off their clothes. Their clothes were whisked away. Their hair was shaved, and then they were directed into a shower. Stella stepped inside, then turned and started to run. Seeing all those shaved heads, she thought the shower was full of men. She didn't understand that all the other women had had their heads shaved too. Her cousin Sara came after her. "Stella, it's us, we're here."

Afterward a guard pushed them to help themselves to clothes that were piled up on a table. There was no underwear, so they went without.

On the second day they were tattooed: Stella's number was A24409, Renée's A24408. They had to learn the numbers by heart, and in a language they did not understand, because the numbers were their new identity.

Everything had been taken away from them: their parents, their hair, their things. Now their names.

But not their shoes. Stella still had her sandals—for the moment.

She doesn't remember where they slept those first few nights—"more blank spots"—but she does remember what came next. On the third day, they were transferred to Lager B at Birkenau, which was an extension of Auschwitz, three kilometers distant on foot. (Anne Frank would arrive there in early September.) Birkenau, like Auschwitz, was a lifeless, treeless, flowerless, colorless landscape, so profoundly removed in every possible way from Rhodes, the only place Stella had ever lived, the only place she knew, as to feel almost lunar.

As the young women came in through the gates, they saw the guard towers and the barbed-wire fence. They were counted and assigned to barracks. Very quickly they solidified into groups of five—five because that was how they lined up in the early morning for reveille. It was the rule. Their group was Stella, Renée, their cousin Sara Notrica, Lucia Franco (who was Sara Notrica's cousin), and Vittoria Cohen.

"The group was our salvation. In Auschwitz, even in August at four o'clock in the morning, there is cold to die from and then at noon a heat that could fry you. Twice a day, morning and evening, the head of the camp came to count us. The five of us clung together. We took turns changing places, warming the middle ones. Without friends, you could never do this."

Do this: survive. "You had to survive physically and you had to survive mentally. They required different skills."

They were assigned work, pointless work: In the morning they moved bricks from one end of the camp to the other and then in the afternoon they carried them back again. In between they ran to the toilets.

As they walked back and forth, carrying these bricks, they sang, anxiously raising their voices and directing them over fences toward the other barracks, hoping that they would be heard.

> *Mamma, son tanto felice*
> *perché ritorno da te.*
> *La mia canzone ti dice,*
> *che è il più bel giorno per me . . .*

And in Judeo-Spanish, a favorite of their mothers and their aunts, that song from the Juderia, and their youth—

> *Una pastora yo ami*
> *Una ija ermoza . . .*

Surely if their mothers heard *this* song (their mothers or their fathers, or aunts, or uncles, someone from home, anyone from home), they would have responded with a line, a melody, even just a word. But no one did. No song came back. No sounds. "And that's when we began to know that they weren't there."

Began to know because it didn't happen all at once, because they didn't understand all at once. Because no one came to inform them that their parents, their aunts and uncles, the parents and aunts and uncles of their friends, had all been murdered.

"Was there never a precise moment when you understood, definitively understood?" I ask Stella.

"That is a question from this world, Michael, not that world. Not only was there never a moment I can pinpoint when I understood, there was never a moment, not for a very long time, when I allowed myself, when any of us allowed ourselves, to *feel*. We were too busy trying to survive." She pauses. "But it was there, of course, everywhere, all the time. This knowledge. It was like a flame. Too ferocious to come near. If we touched it, we might ourselves die."

One of the first things that Stella stopped doing, she tells me, was thinking. Thinking about what had happened to everyone who was missing, but thinking, also, about what might happen to her and the other young women from Rhodes. It was too dangerous to think. If you thought there, in that place, as many people did, many intelligent people did, if you thought to yourself, *We are being treated worse than animals, animals at least you give food to, and water to . . .* if you thought like this you let yourself go and you died, or you killed yourself.

"It was only later that I allowed myself to speculate whether, at the end, my father spoke to God. My mother who even at the Turkish bath did not feel well, couldn't breathe sometimes, who when she felt one of her migraines coming on would hurry out of the Juderia and go to the lighthouse, which was maintained by a Turkish friend of hers, and scramble up the stairs so that she could look out over the open sea, what did she feel in the gas chamber, did she panic, did she faint, did *she* feel the presence of God?"

Many years later a girl in Madrid asked Stella, "After Auschwitz, do you believe in God?" And Stella answered, "If you're asking me whether

God was there, this is not a matter for God, but for man. It was not God, a god, who made this place, it was man."

After she tells me this, Stella disappears into one of her silences. Then she says, "Very early on, almost from the beginning, something curious happened. I detached myself from the Stella who was in Auschwitz. It was as if everything that was happening to her was happening to a different Stella, not the Stella I was, not the Stella from Rhodes, the Stella I knew. I watched this person, this other Stella, as she walked through this desert, but I was not this person."

After a moment she adds, "There was no other way."

63

The barracks they were assigned to had two separate rooms for the (female) *Blockälteste* (barracks leader) and the *Stubenälteste* (room leader), a woman named Magda who woke them in the mornings by pinching them, whip in hand, and grudgingly served them "coffee" that among themselves they called *acqua sporca*—dirty water (it was made from chicory). Both the *Blockälteste* and Magda were Polish Jews. Stella describes Magda as *matta*, crazy, or mentally ill. One morning early on, Sara, herself *matta*, though in an altogether different sense, couldn't take it anymore and threw the *acqua sporca* at Magda, who chased her out of the barracks. Magda had to come back again to do her work—she too was a prisoner, after all—but from that day on she hissed at the young women from Rhodes.

When Stella went back to see the camp in 2004 and mentioned Magda, the tour guide said, "You were in the barracks with Magda? Everyone talks about her." Stella told the guide that she had heard that people tried to track her down after the war. The guide said, "I understand people used to fantasize about being liberated and tearing her to pieces."

· · ·

The other women in their barracks, all Ashkenazi, started to speak to the Rhodeslis in Yiddish and, because Stella and her group didn't understand, couldn't understand, the Ashkenazi Jews didn't believe they too were Jews.

Then came the first Friday night. One of these Ashkenazi women had managed to fabricate two candles from margarine and (for wicks) thread picked out of a fraying blanket. With them that evening was their friend Fortunée Menasce, who was older than they were, twenty-seven or so, and one of the other prisoners asked her, and somehow Fortunée understood, if she knew how to bless the candles. It was a test. She passed.

"So you *are* Jews," they said—or, at any rate, Stella deduced that was what they said.

These other Jews, the Ashkenazi Jews, would become friendlier after that, though Sara whispered to her, "Don't be *that* friendly, they're all thieves." Which is quite funny when you think about it, Stella points out, because they would all become thieves before long, one way or another: "Sara's mistrustfulness was part of her courage. She had the courage to remain a wary human being."

As for Stella, the camp Stella quickly became unrecognizable to the Stella of Rhodes. Overnight, it seemed, she turned into someone who robbed, cheated, connived, was suspicious, vigilant, devious, sly—she did whatever it took to keep herself going every day, and her sister, and her friends. "It was as if I was living by some kind of survival instinct that I didn't know was in me."

Only it was in her, was it not, nascent and developing during the events of the preceding months? On Rhodes she foraged for food on the black market and offered to take her father's place when he was first arrested; on the boat she asked the captain for a lemon for Miriam, and for that swim; on the train she staked out the best corner, she made a connection to the Italian soldier, and she dared to ask if she could wash her hair. These seem like clear signs of someone who was instinctively, intuitively resourceful.

"In Auschwitz, instinct became everything," Stella says. "But instinct wasn't always enough."

64

A number of girls from Rhodes died fairly quickly, many of them, in Stella's estimation, stronger than she was. Luna Gabriel, a champion swimmer, was one; her leg swelled up. It was the first time Stella had heard the word *phlebitis*. They took her to the *rewir*, the infirmary, and that was it. Her younger, less robust sister Clara, who was a friend of Stella's, survived. Matilde Capelluto, a schoolmate of Stella's, woke up with a fever one night and began to scream: "She went out of her mind." Magda took her away, and she was never seen again.

Several others died of diarrhea, either caused by starvation or by drinking the water, which Stella and her group understood early on was dangerous. "We were thirsty more than we were hungry," Stella says, "but still we knew better than to drink the water."

The Auschwitz-Birkenau website explains what was going on:

> A characteristic camp illness was starvation sickness. It was usually accompanied by diarrhea (often bloody), swollen legs, impaired vision and hearing, memory loss, nervous breakdown, and, above all, exhaustion to the point of collapse. The majority of prisoners suffered from several medical conditions simultaneously.

Starvation sickness: When I read this to Stella, she says, "What happened to our bodies, it caused you to lose your humanity. The person who had entered the camp was now a form of human being who did things that were no longer human. It only took a week."

Lying in bed at night, trying to habituate to a state of hunger that was so profound and to them so unprecedented that it really should have gone by a different word, one or another of the young women would speak into the darkness: *Do you remember on Friday when Mamma made* burekas? or *My aunt's* travados *were the best I ever tasted, I wonder if she ever shared the recipe with anyone, I wonder what it was about them that made them so delicious,* and then someone else would say, *Stop, please, you* must *stop talking about this, you will drive me mad,* and the voices would recede and the night, the long night, would draw on, until the next night, or another night, someone would begin again: *Do you remember . . .*

Stella, lying there quietly, thought to herself, *I must put these memories, these associations, out of my mind. It is the only way.*

From one month to the next many of the women's periods disappeared. Stella speculates that something was put into the soup they were given, to suspend their cycles. More likely, though, it was a combination of trauma and malnutrition.

Every week they were disinfected with some kind of chemical: up front, up the behind, under their arms.

One condition that disappeared overnight, Stella tells me, was Renée's asthma, along with her delicateness in general. Overnight? Stella can't mean this literally, can she? "If you want to cure asthma," she says caustically, "go to a concentration camp."

65

The deaths of so many healthy young women, Stella believes, is one of the reasons the *Lagerälteste* (the camp leader) put them with the French women—the story she told me the first evening we sat down next to each other at Casa Italiana: "She wondered why so many girls from Rhodes died so quickly, within days of arrival. In fact, by asking us what languages we spoke, the *Lagerälteste* did, I've come to see, a noble thing. She made it possible for us to understand the rules and what we were being told to do."

The French women, several of whom were in fact from Belgium, were: Madame Katz and her daughter Paula; Madame Levy; Ida and Minuche, who were two sisters; Flor; and Miriam. *Madame* was reserved for the older women, who were perhaps forty, not even. They were surprised that the girls from Rhodes spoke French until they explained about Alliance. The girls from Rhodes and the French women were assigned work duty together. One morning, as they were moving those bricks from one end of the camp to the other, Madame Katz said to them, "*Avez-vous vu les cheminées?*" And she pointed at the chimneys and the smoke rising out of them. If she were a character in a novel, Stella tells me, this might be the moment when she definitively *realized*, but in her actual experience it was merely another piece of information she layered over all the other pieces. Her focus was elsewhere: on how to hold on to her slice of bread. She had recently realized it was best to sleep with it under her ear. The same with a potato, because the other prisoners stole everything, as her cousin had said. "Only it wasn't stealing. It was surviving."

Having a language, being able to communicate again, and to comprehend, made life in the camp more navigable. "It concerned me a great deal not to understand German," Stella says. "Not to follow what we were being told to do or what was going on or happening to us—it put us at constant risk."

The French women shared their knowledge: drink coffee (well, chicory) instead of the water, because at least it was boiled; never complain about illness or toothache; and never ever agree, as some of their friends had, to go to the *rewir*; learn to make do, to make everything work for them.

The first word Stella learned in German was *organisieren*, in Yiddish *organisir*: to organize. It was a word, a concept, that in Auschwitz carried a great deal of weight. It meant making do, making everything work for them, learning to steal (everything possible), to barter (food for shoes, for underwear), to hide, to reinvent objects and maximize resources, to collaborate with people you believed you could trust. Also to repair shoes with wire, to use newspaper for padding, and to take care of themselves by outwitting their minders and the less honest of their fellow prisoners.

Sara was brilliant on this front, and a little reckless too. At Lager B a fence separated the women from the men, and Sara happened to learn that her younger brother Salvo (Salvatore) was there on the other side, among other men from Rhodes, including Sami Modiano and a cousin of Stella's.

The fences were electrified: in a different camp a mother tried to see her daughter—how they became separated was unclear—and she was electrocuted.

Somehow Salvo was able to get word to his sister that he was cold at night. Early one morning, quite by chance, Sara saw a truck going by that was packed with clothes. She caught up with it, climbed in and grabbed a sweater, and pulled it down. A guard positioned in one of the towers saw her and sounded the alarm, commanding everyone in the lager to go inside while Sara was whisked away. "We waited for two hours," Stella says. "They were some of the most awful hours of my life. We were convinced she was killed."

Improbably Sara returned: "When we saw her, you could not believe our screams, we nearly fainted."

To Sara they said, "*Locas sos?*"—Are you crazy?

I ask Stella: *Was* Sara crazy, or was she courageous?

She thinks for a moment before answering both, then she explains Sara's attitude: *The worst they can do is shoot me.*

She was lucky they didn't. Instead she was made to sit outside for the entire day with a roof tile on her head.

66

The following week I come with some very basic questions.

What did their meals consist of?

At breakfast they were served that *acqua sporca*. Odious.

At lunch: soup—with always the first portions the more watery ones since those at the bottom of the pot had a richer accumulation of vegetables and (occasionally) meat.

At dinner: bread with *companatico*—whatever one was given to eat *con pane*, "with bread," a slice of salami for example, or a crust of cheese.

Sometimes the lunch and dinner "menus" would be swapped. "You can't really call them meals. We were animals, reduced to thinking about food all the time."

How did they sleep?

In wide bunk beds three levels high, the upper two reached by hoisting and climbing, on mattresses that were essentially sacks stuffed with straw. Five people slept in each of these beds. "The main thing was to sleep with your bread and your shoes under your head. If one person turned, so did the other. Sleep was not easy, to put it mildly."

Where did they go to the bathroom?

In an enormous cement room with a platform, also made of cement, that had holes cut into it, one after the other in a row. "You had to wait for someone to leave, and then you climbed up and did your business. It was probably my most disgusting memory of Auschwitz. Men were always cleaning while we were emptying ourselves out. Always. A French guy laughed at us."

They returned for showers once a week. They were given small pieces of black soap to wash with, made of what, Stella has no idea. There were no towels.

Did they brush their teeth? "Never. Primo Levi asked if he might have his toothbrush back, and he was told, '*Vous n'êtes pas à la maison*'—you're not at home."

Was carrying bricks from one place to another the only kind of work assigned? "The main one, and I never figured out the purpose of it. Were they testing us to see if we were strong? Trying to drive us mad? It made absolutely no sense."

A choice job, she adds, if you spoke German, was in Canada, which was the name given to the building in which prisoners sorted all the clothes that people brought with them to the camp and immediately had confiscated; items of any quality were separated out and sent to Germany. The place was called Canada because everyone believed Canada was a rich country.

Stella "bought" a sweater for Renée from someone who worked in

Canada—which also supplied goods to the camp's black market—by paying with bread she and Renée had saved up between them: three pieces. This was also how she bought herself some underwear, using salami instead of bread. And clogs to wear once her sandals fell apart. "We worked together as a group, taking turns forgoing bread or *companatico*. It was teamwork."

After a pause Stella adds, "The women, you know, seemed to do better in the camps than the men."

Why was that?

Stella has thought a lot about this question, she tells me. She believes it has to do with women making and carrying life: "Instinctively you protect and preserve your body." By contrast, Stella refers to the *muselmänner* that Primo Levi describes as the drowned, the men who

> form the backbone of the camp, an anonymous mass, continually renewed and always identical, of non-men who march and labor in silence, the divine spark dead within them, already too empty to really suffer. One hesitates to call them living: one hesitates to call their death death, in the face of which they have no fear, as they are too tired to understand.

Stella observed men like these in nearly all of the camps she passed through. "The Germans could have just shot them," she says, "but they knew they would die anyway in a day or two. Why waste the bullets?" They had even ceased interesting their persecutors. "I saw men I knew to have had great strength, mental and physical, who simply couldn't do it."

This was especially true of intellectual men, Stella believes, possibly because they tried to think their way through what was happening to them, or because they were incapable of detaching themselves. "Women never let themselves go like that. We robbed to eat, as soon as our hair began to grow we washed it as best we could, we bartered and bargained. We understood *organisir*, we lived by it, because of it. We did whatever it took to keep going, to keep from, well, succumbing."

This included singing. Even after they gave up any hope of their parents hearing them, the young women continued to sing. They sang in the barracks, while picking the lice out of their resprouted hair. They sang while they worked. They sang to keep themselves distracted, to push down the fear. *La pazza* Miriam (in this case, good crazy, ebullient crazy), would say, "Come, let's hear your Italian songs!" And so they would dive in, with *Mamma, son tanto felice* and, surfacing again, *Tornerai,* and *Triste domenica,* which was originally a Hungarian song—

> *Questo aspettare*
> *vuol dire soffrire,*
> *morire d'amore*
> *per ogni domenica . . .*
> *. . . Triste domenica*

Only the lyrics, they learned, were about a suicide, and it emerged that one of the Hungarian girls knew a young woman who in Budapest had committed suicide soon after the song came out. *Please,* they were told, *sing anything but that.*

Also: they laughed. The jokes, the humor were black, biting, "the kind of humor you find in a play by Samuel Beckett."

This is something, Stella says, that few people tell you. Things were so ridiculous they couldn't stop laughing at them, they couldn't help but laugh at them, though it was laughter accompanied by a dark halo, like gallows humor or when people start laughing at a funeral. "You'd put on a long sock with a short one. They gave you a dress but it was a blouse, and half your underwear, once you had some, *if* you had some, would show. Either the Germans did this kind of thing intentionally or things were just out of the norm, out of whack, out of this world. The camp was out of this world. It was like nothing else we'd ever lived. The absurdity extended to every last detail of daily life. The absurdity and the terror."

Death was always there, front and center in their consciousness. When people fell ill, or died, the Germans gave the orders that the Jews should take the bodies either to the gas chamber or to the crematorium, so that no one ever for a moment forgot what danger they were in. "Death was like this," Stella says, forming her hands into two pointing fingers, two pistols, each poking, repeatedly poking, a side of her face. "It was relentless. They used it, the threat of it, to express their power, to remind us that we were no longer human beings with free choice but captives who had no control over our fate."

67

At the end of October, two and a half months after they arrived at Auschwitz-Birkenau, the women underwent a second selection. This time they were naked. They lined up in front of a man—she has no idea who it was, though people whispered that he was a doctor. In his hand he held a stick. The stick directed them toward life or toward death.

They had experience by now; they had accrued knowledge. When they learned that the selection was coming, Sara hurried to the kitchen and stole a beet, which she passed among all the girls. They rubbed the beet juice into their cheeks, in order to make themselves look pink and healthy.

"Do you think I'll pass?" Renée whispered to Stella. Then: "I won't pass."

"We will pass," Stella told her. It didn't matter what she believed, she said it anyway.

One by one they stepped up to this man.

"I was afraid to look behind me, to look to the side," Stella says. "But I did see, ahead of me, Allegra Avzaradel, a girl from Rhodes who was older than me by two years, she was in Renée's class and perfectly healthy. She had a defect: as a child, she'd been burnt and had a scar on her face—a notable scar, large and impossible to cover up. For this reason alone she was sent to the ovens."

After Stella passed, she felt someone touch her on the shoulder. It was Renée. "That was how I knew she made it too."

So did all the girls in their group of five. In the showers they fell into one another's arms.

They were given new clothes, as usual at random. A coat was included this time, essential because they were heading to Germany. They were to travel by a regular passenger train that was old and shabby, but at least not a cattle car. The train was going to take them to one of the eleven sub-camps of Dachau at Landsberg, known also as Kaufering. Inmates died here, but they were not death camps so much as work camps, established the previous June to use the prisoners as laborers in the production of German aircraft, which had been devastated by Allied bombing.

As they were stepping onto the train, a German guard said to Madame Katz, "You may allow yourselves to hope now."

68

From the train, Stella noticed the landscape changing. Eventually they rode into a forest, whose canopy became thicker and greener the farther they journeyed. The air looked clearer, cleaner too. They traveled through the night and into a part of the next morning, disembarking at the station of Landsberg as if it were a regular travel day.

It was not. "When we stepped down off the train people regarded us as—as animals. Or performers. The way you look at people on a stage, or in the circus."

Landsberg, nevertheless, felt like an entirely different world from Auschwitz-Birkenau.

"In Birkenau you were in a desert, even if it was full of people," Stella explains. "It didn't have the feeling of a place that was alive. That's because it wasn't alive, it was desolate. Landsberg was surrounded by stands of pine trees."

When they arrived, the barracks for the women were still empty and only gradually filled up. Stella and her friends weren't given mindless work here but what felt like actual jobs. Either they were assigned to cleaning the men's barracks while the men were off at work, or they were put on kitchen duty.

Stella worked in the kitchen, stirring cauldrons of soup that were so large that only she and Sara, who were both tall, could reach them. "You could eat what you wanted," she says. "Boiled potatoes. The soup. Not so much meat, though Sara, being Sara, stole a piece once—hot meat, which she hid in her armpit."

Stella demonstrates by standing up and walking with her arms rigidly by her side, like a toy soldier, like Chaplin's little tramp.

"I told Sara if she were caught she could be killed. She said, 'No one will catch me.'"

No one did. A young man who stole a piece of cheese wasn't so lucky. He was found out, and they strung him up and hanged him where everyone could see.

On the third or fourth day in Landsberg the Kapo took Stella into the barracks of German soldiers to clean. While she was working an officer approached her and said something like, "*Sprechen?*" and she answered, "*No deutsch.*" Either it was the language, or her timidity, but nothing happened after that, except that she continued cleaning, and cleaned well. The next day the Kapo sent her back to the kitchen to peel potatoes. It took her a while to understand that the officer likely wanted more from her than housework.

One morning they woke up, early as always, for reveille, and they couldn't open the door to their barracks, which were partially underground. "We thought that they had locked us in, we thought something dreadful was about to happen," Stella says. "We thought they were going to kill us. We started screaming, crying. A wave of panic rose over every last one of us."

They couldn't open the door because in the night snow had fallen against it.

With effort they managed to push the door open, finally, and pour outside.

As Stella stood in line to be counted, she watched the snowflakes land in the branches of the trees. It was the first time in her life that she'd seen snow fall.

69

There wasn't sufficient work for all these young women at Landsberg. By Christmas they were on the move again and separated for the first time since they arrived in Auschwitz. Sara and Lucia (who were cousins, Stella reminds me) remained at Landsberg, while Stella, Renée, Vittoria Cohen, and other girls from Rhodes were transferred to another camp, Türkheim, where they arrived on Christmas and were fed split-pea soup. Diarrhea immediately followed.

Conditions at Türkheim were rougher, and the men were in poor condition. The German soldiers were gone; only a few SS men were there and some older men from the Organization Todt, a civil and military engineering group known for their use of forced labor (during the later years of the war they were responsible for the construction of the camps and supplying labor to industry). The Kapo of the men's camp was from Salonika, having risen up, like many of his fellow prisoners who endured, because of his ruggedness. Primo Levi describes the Jews from Salonika as tenacious, thieving, wise, ferocious, and united, "determined to live, such pitiless opponents in the struggle for life," a take that Stella echoes: "The ones I met had worked at the port. They were strong, physical, protective of each other. They had formed deep bonds among themselves that I'm certain sustained them."

The women who had been there for a long time, some of them from Rhodes, regarded the newcomers with suspicion. Were they going to take their place? Were they going to disrupt the *equilibrium*—Stella uses the English—that they had established with the men from Salonika?

When I ask her what she means by *equilibrium*, she explains that some men and women were having relationships in the camp, in secret.

With each other and also with the guards. This was how several of them landed the better, indoor jobs. A different way of sustaining themselves.

Stella and her group were given the task of moving bags of cement from one place to another. "It was not pointless work, and nor was it hard work," she says. One of the men watching over her, *un vecchietto*—an old guy—gave her an apple every day, and one afternoon he brought her two *choux à la crème*, which she promptly divided up among all her friends. Paula, who read the gesture correctly, said to her, "Do you want to take a walk with him?" Stella answered, "Not that kind of walk."

At Türkheim it was so cold that Stella's eyelashes froze. "In Auschwitz they killed you, in these other camps you died of illness. You had to adapt all the time to new circumstances: weather, people, rules, human dynamics. If your brain isn't strong enough to make a quick switch, to see each new reality the way it is, you perish," she says. "The people who thought, *Basta, we are in hell, we will die*, they do not have the survival instinct."

She pauses and then adds, "I say this and yet I know that I also had luck. Every survivor has a moment, two moments, ten moments of incredible luck." Surviving, she tells me, has as much to do with luck as anything else. "One thing it has nothing to do with is heroism—this word, this notion, is completely at odds with what the experience of the camps was like. We stole, we cheated, we organized, we slept with our bread under our pillows *and* fate treated us kindly. Why should Alice Tarica pass and not her older sister, who was my age? Why did I survive when I wasn't stronger than Luna Gabriel or any of the others? This is how I came to understand about *suerte*."

Stella's, all the young women's, moments of chance and luck were lifesaving, but they were spread out, she reminds me, among long hours of hunger, numbness, senseless hard labor, anxiety, and confusion that unfolded in extreme temperatures and in conditions that were bug-plagued and filthy, during which each of them knew that their lives were of negligible value to their captors and could end just like that—if they stole a piece of cheese or a sweater to keep themselves or a sibling warm, or because they looked into the wrong person's eyes, or for no reason at all except that a man passed by and felt like pulling the trigger on the gun in his pocket.

When she describes life in the camps, Stella will often laugh. When she first did this I thought it was at that Beckettian absurdity, the mismatched socks and unpredictable behaviors and all of that. But it happened so often that I began to wonder whether it was only by laughing that Stella could find a way to bypass the pain, put these experiences into words, and transmit these words across the room in real time, at this time in her life.

More than once Stella has spoken to me about the Stella of Rhodes, whom she detached from soon after she arrived at Auschwitz. But there is a still different Stella, I think, who lurks in—or, more precisely, is excluded from—all the stories that this Stella has told me about her experience of the camps: the Stella who could so easily have been among the 90 percent of those Rhodeslis who perished in Auschwitz and the other camps, the one who didn't have these multiple experiences of luck, the one who didn't survive to tell the tale. That Stella has no stories to tell; this Stella has no lack of them. That Stella is far more representative of what happened to the 1,650 people deported that day in July; this one, the exception, offers accounts from the abyss that, no matter what, end positively, because this Stella is *here*.

That Stella haunts this Stella. How could it be otherwise?

In December 1944 and January 1945, the last of the deportees arrived, Hungarians from Budapest. They couldn't go to Auschwitz because the Russians were nearby—in fact the Russians would liberate the camp at the end of January, on the twenty-seventh. Stella was at work when these women appeared, dressed in fur coats and fur hats, "with an elegance that took my breath away." They came from Budapest in their best winter finery, which was, of course, immediately taken from them. The only clothes available were striped uniforms. Into them they went. Their heads were not shaved.

"The insanity of continuing to deport people when you are losing the war . . ."

At Türkheim they regularly saw American planes flying overhead. "You heard them from far away, *boom boom boom* and then, when they were in retreat, *brrr, brrr.* We were told to go into the barracks, but we stayed outside to watch. We screamed up at the sky, 'Bomb us! Destroy the camps!'"

No one bombed them. No one destroyed their camp. Instead, with the arrival of the Hungarians, the barracks became crowded, and it was time to move on, yet again.

70

In March they arrived in the next camp, another satellite of Dachau that had only a number—Stella thinks it was 21, or 23.

The lager-of-no-name was ruled over by a pair of German women, Erica and another woman whose name Stella has lost, or willed out of her brain. She calls her instead *La Cattiva*, "the mean one," because she screamed at them and used a whip to keep them in line. Both Erica and La Cattiva they addressed as Fräulein. Erica was maybe twenty-eight, blonde, with red cheeks, healthy, "that kind of German." La Cattiva was thin, with dark wiry hair and narrow eyes.

That red-cheeked, healthy kind of German, Erica, would see Stella and the other girls returning from picking potatoes, their job at the time, not so much walking as waddling because of all the potatoes they'd concealed in their pants, which where bulked up and heavy and tucked into their socks, and she would smile, whereas when La Cattiva was on duty they would not dare to steal a morsel, they would rather die of hunger, they would go a day, two, three days without supplementing the camp food. They had seen what she did to a girl who stole: made her kneel all night in the snow.

Erica was different. Erica loved them because they were Italian: "Italian—beautiful," she said. Erica had a favorite among them: Alice Tarica, who at thirteen was the youngest and had blue eyes, like Erica's. When Erica heard them singing—

Ba, ba, baciami piccina
Con la bo, bo, bocca piccolina
Dammi tan, tan, tanti baci in quantità . . .

—like a child, she would ask for more: "*Singt, singt.*"

They danced here too. Miriam, *la pazza* (another crazy one) would say, "*Allons y, les italiennes, on va danser La Cumparcita.*" And while some girls were picking the infernal lice out of their scalps, others would, yes, get up and dance.

In this camp the women's and men's latrines were separated by a single wall, made of wood, that had enough of a space below to pass goods back and forth. Stella and her group traded potatoes with the men for scraps of wood that they used to light the little stove on which they cooked the purloined potatoes. In this way, Stella tells me, they traded also for a knife to slice the potatoes and a spoon to eat them. At the mention of a knife, I cock my head, and Stella says tartly, "How do you think we ate otherwise? You think they gave us cutlery, like in a hotel?" But she has misread my expression; I am thinking back to the day that she and her friend Bella went to lunch at the Menasces and saw that the table had been laid with a knife, instead of just a fork.

As for a spoon, if you were lucky enough to come into one, she adds, you tied it to your leg—it was your single most precious possession.

One day they slipped their potatoes under the wall. The potatoes were whisked away, but nothing came back in return. "I want to kill that man," Sara said, and Stella said, "But you don't even know what he looks like."

71

They came back from work one evening to find Renée, who had returned ahead of them, distraught. When Stella asked her what happened, she said that they took her number down and planned to send her to another camp the next day, one of the camps people didn't come back from.

Stella hurried to Madame Katz and said, "We've been together since we arrived here, my sister and I, and we cannot be separated, it's impossible. We must find Erica, right now we must find her, we must *say* something, we must *do* something." It was after curfew, but they went to the gate and made such a noise that Erica came out of her room, in her nightshirt, and with a wrap, and she said, "Italian, what's going on?" and in German Madame Katz explained. Erica took down Renée's number, went into the office, and changed it for another.

I say to Stella, "Just like that, Renée's fate was substituted for someone else's?"

"Just like that," she says.

"Do you remember what you felt?"

Stella tells me this story on more than one Saturday. One time she answers that she felt nothing, only relief that her sister was saved. Another time she tells me that she felt *vergogna*.

I know what *vergogna* means, but I ask her to define it for me.

"Between guilt and shame. More than each, maybe even more than both together."

After a third telling, I say again, "Just like that, it happened, one person's fate was substituted for another's. What did you feel?"

"You're asking questions that don't make sense to that time and that setting. My goal was to survive, to have my sister survive. The only way for us to survive was for us to stay together."

She pauses, then looks me in the eye. "'We should beware of the errors of judging eras and places according to the prevailing standards of here and now.'"

"Primo Levi?"

She nods, then says, "The here and now are far, far away from the then and there."

72

Stella's hair was beginning to grow back, and one evening, in an unending battle against lice, she managed to wash it. She went outside afterward in the cold air and caught pleuritis. Even though Madame Katz and the other French women had warned her, all of them, repeatedly, never to go near the *rewir*, Stella was so ill that she went anyway. The doctor there was, fortunately, another French speaker, Belgian and also Jewish, with short black hair and wire-rimmed glasses; surely she would be able to give Stella something to make her feel better.

Stella looked longingly at the hospital beds, but after the doctor examined her and gave her an injection, she said to the nurse, "This one does not stay." Under her breath she told Stella she could not risk spending the night there. She must go sleep in the barracks, no matter how ill she felt.

The next morning they emptied out the hospital and took everyone in it to Dachau to be gassed.

This transport of the sick turned out to be part of a larger plan and had to do with a feeling in the air that something was coming. Or rather, someone: the Americans. The question was when.

At reveille they were told to collect their blankets; they were setting off that very day on a march. The destination: Allach, another satellite camp of Dachau, though Stella and the others didn't know it at the time. No one ever told them anything, ever. Not about where they were going or what was about to happen to them. When a German officer ordered them to march, they marched. When he ordered them to stop, they stopped.

Nevertheless people whispered, they spread rumors: They were going to be freed. They were going to be abandoned along the road. They were going to be shot.

They set out under a heavy rain. Stella pushed herself forward, one effortful step at a time. The ground was thick with mud and soupy. Her body was burning and shivering with fever and chills. It rained all day. It rained at night, soaking their blankets. She was never warm or dry. She couldn't stop coughing. She scarcely slept.

The following afternoon they came to a place, a field, where in the distance several barns flashed at her like beacons. Stella looked at them longingly. "I'll stay here and rest," she said to Renée. "I'll hide here, maybe I'll make it to one of those barns . . . maybe they'll give me something to eat . . . maybe I'll sleep or maybe I'll die. You go on without me."

Renée said one word: "*No.*"

Renée, the formerly sickly one, held up Stella, who was truly sick, weak and febrile, and pushed her forward, step by step, until three days later they reached their destination.

Renée, Stella tells me, never again spoke about what she'd done. Not then, or afterward.

As they were marching to Allach, Stella, Renée, and Vittoria were reunited with Sara and Lucia: "How we screamed when we saw them again."

They continued in a now lightening rain. For nourishment they had crusts of bread and whatever *companatico* remained. When they needed to relieve themselves, they would form a circle to create a bit of privacy.

The guards stayed with them the whole time, but other soldiers wove in and out of the moving mass of people. Many of them dropped their weapons and shed their uniforms and with them, they hoped, their identity as soldiers. Then they began hearing the planes—a *zoom* overhead, followed by the whistle of falling bombs. American planes, it turned out, dropping bombs on Munich.

73

The camp at Allach was populated by political prisoners, soldiers from Spain and Italy and even Germany; several had fought in the Spanish

Civil War. Jews were among them, but they were by no means the majority. Stella immediately noted that these men took care of themselves. They were eating; they were relatively tidy; their rooms were clean.

Instead of barracks at Allach there were large houses built of cement and furnished with bunk beds. They shared their accommodations with the German guards and had no work to do.

They were there for maybe a week when they woke up one morning to the sound of people screaming, "There are no more Germans!" and "The guards have all left!"

The political prisoners took charge of the camp and organized the food. The moment Stella learned that the Germans were gone, her pleuritis became suddenly, well, less relevant.

She and her friends tried to decide what to do, where to go; Munich, they knew, was the closest city, but they didn't speak German. What was to become of them? They were afraid to leave the camp. They decided to wait.

A day, maybe two days, later, they heard the rumble of jeeps and trucks in the distance. The sound grew louder . . . and then they saw them: American troops. They came driving along the road. They were heading to Dachau; they didn't even know Allach existed.

"We started yelling and screaming. The Americans were surprised to find us; I still remember the looks on their faces, the way their mouths hung open when they saw us, and their eyes, which were wide with—not just surprise but something beyond surprise, astonishment, I guess, at what we had come to, and the condition we were in. We instead just gazed at them in their clean uniforms and crisp combed hair, and we said to each other, 'But they're so tall.'"

The American soldiers threw chewing gum and chocolates over the fence. Just like in the movies.

"Once we realized we were free, we fell to our knees and started weeping. For all we had been, for all that we had lost. We could *feel* things, we allowed ourselves to experience the pain. We came back to ourselves, we became human once more—we didn't have to protect ourselves from life.

In fact afterward we asked ourselves, why all these tears, we weren't sure where they came from, *tutto un miscuglio*"—a big confusion.

"For the first time in these eleven months we finally, truly understood what this thing was. We had left a whole community in the ashes of Auschwitz. It's the reason none of us ever returned to Rhodes to live. Before this day I had never seen one of our girls cry, not from grief. And we had suffered, deeply, inconsolably. But we had never wept."

I ask her why not.

"One of the French women said it to us early on: 'Never cry—it weakens you.' But honestly it wasn't a choice. It just *was*."

One of the American officers took charge of the camp. Soldiers gave them disinfectant soap to shower with, and a nurse and doctor examined them. Stella and the other women were asked to help cook and clean. The Americans had brought canned food and milk, eggs, and orange juice in powdered form, which Stella had never seen before. They were very concerned about the water. Eventually the Red Cross came and took over.

A doctor was there, and right away he said, "Don't give them fat." He knew it could harm them, kill them. When Stella arrived at Auschwitz she weighed 110 pounds; she was under 80 when she was liberated. She heard about men who started eating and eating. Their systems couldn't take it, and soon afterward they died. They didn't die of starvation but from gorging themselves.

Stella asked Madame Katz to teach her how to say *soeur* and *frère* in English. To the Americans she said, "Sister—in America. Brother—in America." They were the first phrases she ever spoke in English.

74

After months, then years, of skirting around the story of her time in the camps, Stella has finally laid it out for me across many Saturdays. I've watched her overcome her resistance, on some days diving in with

relative ease, on others struggling to decide what to share with me, what to hold back. Several times I found myself apologizing for having to ask her to return yet again, or to clarify or amplify what I've heard and registered and done my best to capture as accurately as possible. Often I've wondered what it was like for her after I returned home at the end of one of our Saturdays, leaving behind a difficult swirl of memory.

When we come to this natural pause I ask Stella why she decided to tell me about the camps, after all.

She thinks for a long time before answering, "Because you were patient with me, and because you wanted to know the whole of me." She pauses. "It wasn't easy. There was this . . . this problem, as I see it, that I had to face. It began long before we started meeting. The more you speak, the more the experience becomes yours—it becomes *you.* I didn't want this experience to become part of my life, meaning part of my character, my plasma."

"But wasn't it already part of your life," I say gently, "even when you didn't speak about it?"

"More and more I've come to accept that," Stella says. "But even so, even now, when I speak to you—it's not as though it happened to someone else, it happened to me, but a different me. Someone who lived and saw with different eyes, a different brain. I'm still after all these years trying to understand this woman, fit her back into the outlines of . . . of who I am."

By necessity her brain in the camps, as she has said to me before, narrowed its range. She emptied out any memories of Rhodes as best as she could, because to think about Rhodes was to put herself in danger of failing.

Did she never think about, ask about, the near future? Did she ever say or speculate—to herself or her fellow prisoners or the people in charge, Will this end? Or: How, or when, will this end?

She answers me with a line from Dante, beholding (with Virgil by his side) the entrance of hell: *"Lasciate ogni speranza voi ch'entrate"*— abandon all hope, you who enter. (It's almost the exact opposite, I note, of what the German guard said to Madame Katz as they were leaving

Auschwitz.) Then she adds, "We lived in a perpetual present. We edited out the past and the future equally. It was the only way."

Now it is seventy-five years later, and Stella's thoughts range more freely, to moments that are especially difficult, and across larger themes and spans of time.

Again she tries to picture whether her mother knew what was happening, she and her aunts as they took their last breaths. "Who died first? Who fell to the ground? Did they hold each other? All these things I ask myself now, since I have the possibility of imagining what they could not."

I ask Stella if she is angry. She says, "It's larger than anger, separate from anger. It's a monstrosity that you cannot reason through. You cannot be angry at *all* Germans—though for years I wouldn't go to that country. How can you be angry when I saw, while we were still in Allach, German women in rags dragging their babies and bags along the road, their homes destroyed, their lives ruined? You did not have to be Jewish to suffer through those years. But the Jews . . . the Jews . . . this was something apart."

When they realized that they were free, Stella said, they were ready to return to life.

So quickly? I ask.

"Yes, yes, yes!" she says. "The minute the Americans came we started making our beds, combing our hair as best we could. Just by being there they gave us a taste of the outside world. The men were different, every day another one of them died. I saw the bodies stacked up."

An American officer gave Sara a ride into Munich on his jeep and thrust money into her pocket. All the shops were open. She returned with lipstick.

Sara right away wanted to put on a play, to sing and dance with the Americans: "We were so elated that they weren't the Russians or the English. So we improvised a stage, and we got up on it and we sang and we danced."

75

At Allach Sara met and became involved with a Frenchman. In order to see if the relationship had a future, she accepted a ride to Paris with some Americans who were headed that way. Stella and the rest of the girls thought (and told her) that she was being impulsive, even a bit reckless, "but you know Sara—by now I feel you do."

Sara didn't care what the others thought. It was a way to get out, to get moving. She assured them she'd go to the local Jewish community for help, and she'd get in touch with her brothers who lived in Congo. "I'll be fine," she told them, and in her way she was: the relationship went nowhere, but cousins of cousins took her in, and soon she began a new chapter in her life.

When Stella visited Paris years later she looked up these cousins—who were also cousins of hers, on Miriam's side—and they were still shaking their heads about Sara: *quelle femme.*

After about two more weeks at Allach, Stella and the other women traveled by jeep to Bolzano, the first Italian town beyond the Alps and just inside the border. Stella was to see Italy at long last.

Their driver was Black, the first African American Stella had ever spent time with, though people of color did occasionally pass through Rhodes.

At an army barracks they were welcomed, though with some initial confusion as to whether they were prisoners, which was quickly resolved. They took the first hot showers they had had in a year, with soap too—Stella thinks she must have washed her hair five times—and they were looked after by a team of nuns and volunteers, many of them the daughters of aristocratic families, the *baronessa* this and *contessa* that, who gave them large clean white nightshirts to wear and showed them to a dormitory with comfortable beds and starched sheets, where they promptly passed out from exhaustion, waking only when they heard these curious women at the door, peeking and speculating, and whispering, "*Lascia-mole dormire*"—let them sleep. Only by then the Rhodeslis were awake, pretending to be asleep. They didn't want to leave those beds, they didn't want even to *think* about moving.

Let them sleep: This was the beginning of a pattern that would emerge in those months and early years when people hesitated, or were afraid, or didn't have the vocabulary to ask Stella and the others about their experience in the camps, believing that they were somehow protecting them by not encouraging them to speak. Better that they should rest and recuperate, move forward with their lives, turn their attention elsewhere, went the thinking. The thinking went in this direction for a very long time.

In Bolzano they quarantined for two weeks, all of them remaining in good health, but then the doctors diagnosed a case of typhus elsewhere in the barracks; faced with the prospect of a second quarantine, the young women from Rhodes asked an American soldier for a ride. When he asked where he should take them, they answered: to the nearest city with a Jewish community.

The city was Modena, where the synagogue was shuttered and the caretaker told them that no one had yet returned from hiding . . . or elsewhere. There wasn't a single Jewish person to be found.

"How about Bologna?" the American soldier asked, and they continued on their way.

76

In Bologna, the young women presented themselves at the synagogue. They knew no one. They had no contacts, no papers, no money.

Right away they were taken in by a family called Zuckerman, recently returned themselves from hiding in Switzerland; the oldest daughter, an ardent Zionist, had begun working with Jewish refugees, though she had not yet seen a single actual survivor. Stella, Renée, and the others were in fact among the first—if not the actual first—Italian-speaking Jewish women to return from any of the camps.

"But be sure you put 'return' in quotation marks," Stella says. "Don't forget, it was the first time any of us had seen Italy."

I haven't forgotten.

In Bologna they were taken to a bakery where they sat down, drank coffee, and ate all the pastries they wanted. They were invited to the opera, the first Stella had attended in her life. "Everyone stared at us for the longest time. We were still wearing our American khaki uniforms, so they knew who we were, where we'd come from." Several days later another member of the community, herself just out of hiding, took them to a shop, Jewish-owned, and said, "Dress them all." It was May, and warm, but Stella chose a sweater anyway, "Just to have it."

One afternoon a group of partisan women took Stella and the others along with the Zuckerman daughter to a site at the edge of the city, where resistance fighters, among them several women, had been murdered. Splashes of dried blood stained the walls; the very atmosphere of the place felt charged, almost alive in its lifelessness, and disturbing. The experience shook Stella and stayed with her for years, decades, afterward. Looking back now, she supposes the point was to show them that in Italy not everyone was Fascist, not everyone supported or abetted the regime, that there were in fact Italian men—and women—who gave their lives for democracy and liberty. In a similar vein, later on and for years people would insist on telling Stella about the Italians who had saved, protected, or hidden Jews, and it was true, many had; but there were also Italians who had made lists, cooperated with the Fascists and the Germans, and betrayed their Jewish neighbors. It was difficult, but necessary, to live with both these truths.

Through the Zuckermans the women met members of the Jewish, or Palestinian, Brigade. Formed late in the war, toward the end of 1944, as

part of the British Army, it was made up of Jewish soldiers from Mandatory Palestine; they had fought in the latter stages of the Italian campaign and before returning home were pausing in Bologna. Within minutes after they had been introduced to the young women from Rhodes, one of the soldiers asked Lucia if she had a brother named Nissim; she answered, blanching, that, yes, in fact she did, though she had not seen him in years, given that he had left the island well before the deportation. Well, the soldier informed her, Nissim Franco was part of the brigade, stationed at the moment near the Austrian border. Within days Nissim came to Bologna and was reunited with his sister—he was the first person from Rhodes the young women saw after they were liberated.

Another soldier, a sergeant named Kubrick, saw to it that Stella's brother Morris was informed of his sisters' fate, sending a report in a letter written by a man called Moshe Levin, a faded copy of which Stella digs out of one of her boxes and reads to me:

Bologna, June 10, 1945

Dear Mr. Levi,

By this time you had undoubtedly received already the cable notifying you that your sisters Stella and Renata Levi are alive and well.

Passing through Bologna, I met your sisters last night in the Jewish Community building of Bologna. Both look and feel fine. Of course they will need quite a bit of rest. They were liberated from the notorious concentration camp of Dachau [*sic*] by American troops. They together with four more girls from Rhodes are being taken care of by Sgt. Kubrick of a Palestinian unit with the British Army. It is probable that in the near future they will move to Roma via Firenze. Sgt. Kubrick is doing all that is only humanly possible under the circumstances for them. He will be very glad to hear from you as soon as possible.

After adding Kubrick's address, Levin goes on to say,

> The girls are most anxious to hear from you and your sister in
> San Francisco as well as from the brother in Congo. Yours was
> the only address that they remembered.
>
> I promised the girls that I shall write to you immediately,
> giving in consideration the horrible conditions under which
> they lived for a year their recovery is indeed remarkable.
>
> You can rest assured that the Palestinian soldiers will
> do their utmost for the girls. Those soldiers are doing an
> outstanding work for the Jewish refugees.

I try to picture Morris, receiving the cable, then opening this letter in faraway Los Angeles to read about the fate of Renée and Stella, the two younger sisters whom he'd never met before in his life. Had he heard anything, learned anything, about the fate of his parents? (Who, I wonder, cabled on behalf of the dead?) Or did he deduce from the lack of mention of them, or from the facts about the war as they were becoming known? Clearly at the very least he saw the deep significance of this letter, which he xeroxed and gave to Stella, who has kept it all these years.

77

Rhodes, Athens, Auschwitz-Birkenau, Landsberg, The Camp With No Name, Allach, Bolzano, Modena, Bologna: Where was their odyssey to take Stella and Renée from here?

Not to Palestine, though Sergeant Kubrick had at one point floated the idea.

Not—for a long while—to the United States to meet up with their older siblings, because the sisters had no papers, no visa, no passport: in short, no documents attesting to their identity. And even when they did eventually obtain them, because they were still Italian citizens, and because the United States had severe quotas in place limiting immigrants from Italy, they were repeatedly denied entry in a series of coldly factual letters that Stella also digs out for me to read. ("The misses Levi will have to wait their turn on the quota lists. The fact that they have been interned in a prison [sic] camp does not give them priority for entry.") It would end up taking them more than a year to sort out, and wait out, this bureaucratic tangle.

Should they return, like Odysseus himself, to where they started from, home to Rhodes? Only what sort of Rhodes would that be?

When I ask Stella if she can reconstruct her thinking at this juncture, she brings up Primo Levi: he had his job, his home, his family waiting for him. She did not; nor did any of the others in their group. They had nothing. No one said to them, in these words, "Your Rhodes, life as you knew it in the Juderia, has been extinguished," but she knew, she says, in her soul, that streets, walls, windows, and *kortijos* did not, by themselves, constitute a home. She felt this *vuoto*, this emptiness, in her very body. "My parents were gone, my family, my neighbors, my friends—what would it mean to return to the Juderia? What would that feel like? I was not yet ready to find out. And I wouldn't be for many years."

When, eventually, Alice Tarica's uncle came from Paris to Florence to collect her, he confirmed what they sensed already, what they knew already, that the Juderia was no more. Allied bombing had destroyed many buildings, but it was unclear what had happened to those that remained intact. At first rumors circulated that the Greeks had rushed in to seize whatever food and valuables they could; later it emerged that the carabinieri had collected the contents of Jewish homes and put them in storage.

In their group of young women, several wanted to see for themselves. Rebecca Capelluto went first to Cairo, where her older sister lived, then to Rhodes to find out what, if anything, remained of the family store and to sell the family house. The same for Lucia Franco: on her way home to Kos she stopped in Rhodes, and she too confirmed that there was no there there. Lucia traveled with her Italian boyfriend, Ottorino (Nino) Garzolini, who, in one of several curious coincidences that characterize Stella's life, was the officer who told her, on that awful day in December 1943, that Gennaro Tescione had committed suicide; he and Lucia eventually married and moved to Congo, where they were soon absorbed into the local community of Rhodeslis in exile. In certain ways the warp and weft tightened; in others the fabric was rent for good, forever.

A pattern was followed by many of the Rhodeslis who survived the camps: people hurried to marry and settle down, even those who didn't know each other very well. They wanted normality; they wanted safety; they wanted to be taken care of, or do the caretaking. "They forgot—they *appeared* to forget—what happened in Rhodes, and afterward," Stella says. "How did they do this? I could never understand . . ."

Renée and Stella were different. They took their time. When eventually they did marry, they both married outside of the community.

But this lay in the future. The question at hand, after Bologna, was where to go next—and the answer was obvious: to Florence, where Luigi Noferini was waiting for them. Florence would become Renée and Stella's base while they sorted their papers. Its streets would be Stella's university: for more than a year she would live in them, explore them, and come to know them in the company of her teacher and friend. She would immerse herself in the Italy of her dreams, the one she'd been packed for, and waiting for, since she was fourteen.

78

The logistics, some of them, have faded from Stella's memory. First she thinks the Jewish Brigade drove them to Florence; then she reconsiders and wonders if the Joint Distribution Committee paid for their train tickets, as they did (of this she's more certain) their lodging in Florence. She deduces that Luigi, who worked both as a journalist and a teacher, must have been aware that they were en route, because how else would they have known to go to the Pensione Annalena near the Palazzo Pitti on the Oltrarno, a place where they were so well taken care of over the course of the year they lived there, and where yet another of these Stella coincidences played out, though it would only become clear a lifetime later: at the Annalena she met Emanuele ("Nello") Cassin, a Florentine Jew who had recently emerged from having hidden in various convents and farmhouses to find that his home had been raided by the Fascists then damaged by bombs and artillery fire during the liberation; Nello's grandson Alessandro, the deputy director of Centro Primo Levi in New York, would become a significant friend in Stella's later years. Grandfather and grandson never met, but Stella told parts of her story to both, the first time early, the second late, in her long life.

What Stella does remember vividly is the day that she and a squad of young women—among them Renée, Lucia Franco, Rebecca Capelluto, and Alice Tarica—went to look for Luigi. From the letters he'd written to Stella in Rhodes, she knew that his school was in the *centro storico*, not far from the Baptistery somewhere near via Nazionale, and the day after they arrived in Florence she led the girls across the Arno, one or another of them asking her how she could possibly find it. "There will be a flag or a sign or something," Stella said. "I'll have a feeling." The others lingered, peering into nearly every shop window along the way, so that by the time they reached the neighborhood the school day was winding down and, voilà, almost as if he'd been summoned, there was Luigi, standing on a street corner, speaking to a colleague. The colleague noticed this band of young women wearing American Army–issued khaki and told Luigi to turn around. "The look on his face, the joy in it . . . He sprinted, he *ran*, over to us, and he kissed us, all of us, even those of us he didn't know. He called Renée *piccola donna*—from *Little Women*. He kissed me last. And when he did, he cried."

Luigi, Stella observes, was the first significant person from her life before whom she met afterward.

When I ask her what that felt like, she turns her head away and doesn't answer.

In their first proper conversation that evening, Luigi told Stella and the others that, at the end of the summer of '43, when he'd gone home to visit his family, he'd tried to return to Rhodes, but because he was a communist he'd been forbidden. He knew, eventually, what had happened to them and to the other Jews of Rhodes and spoke of the deep *vergogna* he felt that human beings had been reduced to *this*. The pain he felt with regard to Gennaro Tescione's suicide, he told Stella, was bottomless; he believed that if he'd been there, Gennaro never would have taken his own life.

"How can you be sure of that?" Stella asked him.

"Because if I'd been there, he'd have had a friend nearby."

In Florence, with Luigi as their guide, they saw everything. "Imagine," he said to them as he led them through the city, "here Beatrice walked, here Dante wrote his poetry. Here Michelangelo lived, and painted, or sculpted"—and Donatello, and Frà Angelico, and Frà Bartolomeo, and Giotto, and Botticelli. It was Stella's dream to learn and it was Luigi's to teach. He took them to see work by the della Robbias and Brunelleschi and Alberti. He took them to see the monks' cells at San Marco, the Laurentian Library and staircase, the Medici tombs at San Lorenzo.

To Stella it felt less a rebirth than a birth, full stop. The person she left in the camps was dead (or so she believed, or hoped, at the time), because that person lived merely to stay alive, not to know the world, to see or study or understand the world. When she was first liberated she was a stranger to herself. Who was she? *Where* was she? She no longer had the protection of family or friends or home; she had little in her life that was familiar. She didn't feel anything as simple or straightforward as elated or relieved. In Florence she came not so much back to herself as into a new self. But slowly.

One day Luigi took them to Santa Croce to visit the tomb of Ugo Foscolo, the half-Greek and half-Venetian poet and revolutionary. Foscolo's mother was from Zakynthos, the Ionian island whose 275 Jews had met a starkly different fate from those of Rhodes: ordered by the Germans to present a list of the island's Jewish residents, the mayor and the bishop delivered precisely two names—their own.

"Here are your Jews," the bishop was reported to have said when he did.

Carefully hidden in the remote hills, every single one of these 275 Jews survived the war.

Another day, when one of the first Shabbats rolled around, they decided to attend services at the synagogue. As soon as they walked in Stella gasped: sitting calmly in the sanctuary, waiting for the rabbi to begin, were her second cousin Becky Habib and Becky's mother, Miriam, who was a cousin of Miriam Levi's on the Notrica side. If Nissim Franco and Luigi Noferini were the first people Stella had seen from her life before, Becky and Miriam were the first family she laid her eyes on. And when she did, Stella felt something crack open inside of her.

Becky and Miriam had left Rhodes before the war and wound up in Nice because Miriam Habib's sister Leah had moved there even earlier (they were the daughters of Chaim Notrica, Miriam's uncle who came to the Juderia by limousine to sit shivah for his sister Sara when she died). As the Germans were about to invade France, the local Italian consul advised them to leave the country, and quickly. They went to Italy where, they soon realized, they were no safer. Through friends they found a place to hide in the countryside outside of Florence; now that the war was over they had taken rooms in town and, like the troupe of young women, were trying to decide where to go, what to do next.

"They were the first family members to whom we had to describe what happened to our family," Stella says. It was a step—a small, fragile step—toward integrating (for many years trying to integrate, and often failing) the experience of the camps into their lives.

79

Alice Tarica, the youngest among them to survive the camps, was a twin—her brother was murdered as soon as they arrived, as were the remaining Tarica sisters and their parents—and Stella still can't understand how Alice managed to pass as one of the older girls. She had become very attached to Stella in the months they'd been together. The uncle who came from Paris to collect her might as well have been a stranger. He was, in fact, a stranger: she had never seen him before in her life. He had been desperately combing through lists of survivors. He found her name and tracked her down; he was determined to look after his only surviving relation.

Alice's leave-taking was very emotional, but she went, and some years later married—no surprise!—a second cousin of Stella's and moved to Congo. Rebecca left next, then Lucia, and finally Vittoria. Of their band of young women only Renée and Stella remained behind. In order to obtain a passport they had two choices: to return to Rhodes or to apply in Naples. They chose to do the paperwork from Naples, no matter how long it took.

Luigi introduced them to Tescione's father, Giovanni, who was also a lawyer, and offered to help them sort out the bureaucracy. When I ask Stella why it took as long as a year, at first she answers tartly, "Ask the Italian government." Then she adds that the Italian government was just beginning to function again, and they were far from the only people without papers. The Americans weren't exactly making it easy either—the opposite.

Leaving Renée at the Annalena, Stella made frequent trips to Rome, where she took a room at a pensione in the Piazza del Popolo and fell in with other young Rhodeslis who had returned from the camps and lived in a kind of group home in the via dei Condotti that had been loaned to, and was overseen by, a woman called Vittoria Cohen (another Vittoria Cohen) and her husband, Angelo. In Rhodes this Vittoria had been a seamstress, struggling to get by; in Rome, with charity backing, she reinvented herself as a housemother to these homeless young women (and some men, though they lodged elsewhere) and helped make Stella feel comfortable in the big city. As Florence had been, now Rome became part of Stella's education, the Italy she had been waiting all her life to know.

The year in Italy gave Stella ample time to think about Luigi. What began as a mentor-pupil relationship that had, as Stella once described it, its Brontë-esque aspect now evolved into a more mature, and balanced, rapport. Luigi introduced Stella to his family, who though they'd never before met a Jewish woman (or man either, for that matter), gave Stella and Renée a warm welcome and embraced Stella as Luigi's presumed future wife. When eventually the papers came through making it possible for the sisters to travel to the States to see, and in Morris's case meet, their siblings, Luigi, after resisting at first, understood that it was the right thing to do. As a communist, he would have a difficult time accompanying them; he sent Stella off with every expectation that she would return to marry him. "*La piccola donna* can come back too," he said brightly.

Stella, privately, had different ideas. Different feelings. Or maybe at this point they were still inklings. She needed time to think, to work out her life—to *be*.

"I didn't know this quite yet," she tells me, "but I didn't want to be a housewife. Even though he was Luigi, meaning a cultivated man, intelligent and with a big heart, what would my life have been? I'd have become, most likely, a housewife—and I wasn't ready for that."

"Were you in love with him?"

She answers a question with a question: "What does it mean to be in love?"

And then, answering her own question, Stella goes on to tell me that nobody believes that you can love more than one person at a time—but that she knows from experience that it is possible. In Rhodes, she was in love, in her way, as best as she understood "in love," at any rate, with three men: Luigi Noferini, Renzo Rossi, and Gennaro Tescione. Luigi—"if I had to sum it up"—for his intelligence, Renzo for his worldliness, Gennaro for his poetry and his imagination. Looking back now, she says that her strongest feeling was likely for Gennaro, because of the nobility of his soul and the way it spoke to her; the way he spoke to her.

To her mind, love, Stella tells me, can be expressed in many different ways. Sexual attraction and connection, *true* connection, are not always located in the same person. "The person you might want to be intimate with, you might not want to live with. The person you might want to spend time with, take walks with, share ideas and speak with deep into the night, you might not want to be close to physically." She pauses. "Some of my most significant friendships have been with women. I resist the identifying tags that these days people put on everyone, everything. Why must we classify or limit everything with a name, a label, or a category?

"I have a quality of love, and friendship, to offer to many people," she says. "And I have received love and friendship from many people too in my life. It has given me a rich life. In many ways it has *made* my life."

Nevertheless when Stella set off for the States, at least consciously she had every intention of eventually returning to Italy, likely to Florence, to marry Luigi, who was patiently waiting for her the whole time.

80

On November 19, 1946, Renée and Stella traveled to Naples and boarded the *Marine Perch*, destination New York, where it would dock just short of three weeks later, on December 9. "One thing was clear to me as we boarded the ship," Stella says, "and that is that Renée and I had no real idea of what was waiting for us. We were two *orfanelle* who didn't know where to put our heads down, where we would end up."

Not long after settling into their cabin, the two orphans set out to stroll along the deck, where they noticed a chaise longue reserved under the name "Stellina Levy." *Stellina* is a diminutive for *Stella*, and they thought this was curious, especially given that their finances most certainly didn't allow for such luxuries. Was it Luigi's doing? Stella didn't think so, but she couldn't be sure. She and Renée lingered by the chaise for a few minutes, then a few more minutes, and a few more still. Eventually two stylish women approached to claim the seat and the one next to it, which was reserved under the name of another Levy, Fanny.

"Is one of you Stellina Levy?" Stella asked.

"I am!" said one of the women.

"Well, so am I," said Stella.

The two gave each other a hug of greeting—or, rather, meeting.

"But I've seen you two before," Fanny Levy said, after looking at them carefully. "You were at the consulate in Naples."

Yes, they were, Stella answered. Several times, in fact.

Stellina and Fanny were sisters-in-law. Accompanied by the older two of Fanny's five children, they were returning from Milan, where they'd paid their first postwar visit to the city they'd left soon after the racial laws, to check on their homes and their affairs. In New York Fanny and her husband were in the antiques business, with a shop in Manhattan on the East Side in the 60s; Stellina and her husband were furriers on 38th Street. A plain-speaking woman of just under forty, Fanny had a wry sense of humor—she liked to refer to the not-quite-antiques that she and her husband sold to the bourgeoisie of New York City as "Jewish Renaissance"; she was also insightful and embracing, and sometime in the not-too-distant future, Stella tells me in one of her foreshadowings, she would play a decisive role in Stella's fate. When I ask Stella if she'll tell me this story today, she answers with an elfish smile, "I prefer to make you wait."

During the crossing to New York the women did not leave one another's side, except to sleep. And when they arrived, and were about to part ways, Fanny said to Stella, "I feel in my bones that I'll be seeing you again."

In New York Stella and Renée went to stay with cousins in Brooklyn for a week or so, and then they boarded the train for California, where four of the older Levi siblings had settled. They were to be reunited with their family at long last.

81

"What I felt when I saw my brother Morris for the first time at the train station, and Selma, Sara, and Felicie after all these years, *non posso dirti*"—I cannot tell you, or describe for you. So Stella begins the following Saturday.

But then she does just that:

"The tears—on all sides—were unending. They wept and we wept. And it wasn't just because of us, really; or rather, yes, it was because of us *and* because of what we represented. Our arrival in Los Angeles made the tragedy of what happened in Rhodes, and after Rhodes, real to all of them. They cried for the loss of our home, the death of our parents, the end, well, of everything they had grown up with, everything *we* had grown up with . . ."

Like many of the Rhodeslis who had landed in Los Angeles, Morris lived in Leimert Park, and over the next several days anyone who had a connection to the Juderia came there to see Renée and Stella, first among them Miriam's older brother, their uncle Isaac, who had brought Felicie with him to Los Angeles in 1940. Isaac had lost two sisters and a brother in the camps and, like those giants he had once seen by the Puerta de la Mar, had himself become one of *los buenos de mosotros*, the best of them—the best and the only, as he was now also the single member of his generation still alive.

Day after day relatives and friends and friends of friends, came to ask questions. *Did they know what happened to ——? When did they last see ——? Did —— have anything to say at the end? Did —— know that it was the end?*

And they listened intently to the girls' answers. The best answers, that is, that they could give. Sometimes they had none to offer.

The visitors lit candles; they said prayers; they wept. They came and they went, but in the manner of the kindhearted women in Bologna, they didn't ask the sisters about the specifics of their experiences in the camps. "The thinking at the time was, *Why upset us?* So they, and we, remained largely silent."

Sometime after Stella and I have this conversation, I come across an eight-millimeter film that Stella's dedicated archivist cousin Aron Hasson has tracked down, two silent minutes of rich, beautifully mellowed old color footage that captures what appears to be a birthday party held, likely at Morris's house, in early 1947, not long after Stella and Renée arrived in Los Angeles, and I bring this film to Stella. Together we watch a frieze of figures pass across the screen, a mid-twentieth-century version, I can't help but think, of the friezes that depict battles or processions on ancient temples or encircle Greek vases: Levis and Mizrahis, Notricas and Hassons, everyone dressed in party clothes and holding hands or waving or making gestures of greeting, or draping arms across shoulders, or sinking a cake knife into a festively decorated pastry.

Stella and Renée, handsome, glowing, with large orchid corsages pinned to their collars, offer opaque smiles to the camera that are not easy to interpret or, rather, are not easy to separate from everything I know about the long journey that brought these women back into the fold of what remained of their family.

Every few seconds I pause the film so that Stella can put names to faces, link names to names, detail further the cousinage and kinship among these vibrant, enduring Rhodeslis. When we come to the end I realize that one name, one face, one person is notably missing: Felicie.

During these gatherings, the early ones, when they first arrived, and at later ones like this party, Felicie was nowhere to be seen. The first time she disappeared, Stella went to look for her and found that she had retreated into her bedroom and closed the door.

"But why?"

"I asked her myself. Not *why* but *what*. As in: What was she doing in there? And she answered, 'I went to listen to Beethoven's Ninth.'"

Felicie went to listen to Beethoven's Ninth, Stella reasons, because her world had vanished. A world that was built on the thinking and writing of the ancients and was fed by German (and French, and Italian)

music and art, philosophy and novels, comprised an approach to living that hummed through certain streets and certain rooms in the Juderia, the streets where Felicie lived, the rooms where she sat and read and talked deep into the night with Robert Cohen in his mismatched socks, and believed, not in God, not in religion, but in a fundamental human decency—these rooms, this world, which still existed in her mind and memory, were upended by the mere fact of Stella and Renée's presence, by what they embodied, and had lived through.

Listening to Beethoven was all Felicie could do. All she could think, or bring herself, to do.

82

Not long after Stella and Renée arrived they met a man socially, a plastic surgeon who noticed that Renée was hiding her arm, he asked her if she would like to have the numbers removed. "It's not difficult. I can do it."

She made an appointment for the following day for herself and Stella.

What was to come of the two *orfanelle* next?

Renée was twenty-five, Stella twenty-three. Now began a time of bouncing around as they tried to figure themselves out: Where to live, how to live. Where to work. How to find friends. Boyfriends maybe; maybe husbands.

Were they going to follow in Felicie's footsteps?

When Felicie joined Morris in Los Angeles, she had first gone to work as a seamstress—intellectual Felicie, who had never picked up a needle in her life. She was taught to sew by a kindhearted Italian woman who shared the earnings of her own piecework until Felicie caught on, which took some time. Later she ended up taking a job in the office of a retirement home. In the evenings and on weekends she was the always-available aunt, helping look after her nieces and nephews, giving of her time, generous with her money.

"She became the spinster aunt," Stella says, "a dreadful term. We forgot what she had, and so she forgot what she had. She allowed us to take advantage of her, and we did. And we—I, anyway—felt guilty about that, for many years. But the sad truth is that not all gifted or intelligent people give something back, even though it once looked like they might."

As this evaluation of Felicie seems rather harsh, I ask Stella if there might not be another way to frame Felicie's postwar life. The dignity with which she took up manual work—that was impressive. And her financial generosity seems quite significant too. When I point this out, Stella concedes that Felicie was the first person to send her sisters money while they were in Florence and that for many years afterward she helped (even bailed) them out at several important crossroads in their lives. The money leads to other aspects of Felicie's generosity: where she chose to direct energy, efforts, and beliefs. Once Felicie moved to Berkeley, she joined demonstrations for civil and women's rights and against the war in Vietnam. She became involved in union organizing. The young woman who had spoken critically—or whispered, safely after dark—about the Fascist regime now raised her voice against aspects of the government of her adopted country that struck her as unjust.

And eventually, although she remained disinclined to talk to Renée or Stella about their experience of the camps, Felicie read a great deal about the subject. "She wanted to understand—to try to understand—philosophically, but of course in the end she couldn't, as who could? And she felt guilty: for being the last of us to leave, for not being there to help when our father lost his work, his vision. I think if she had left earlier, like Sara or Selma, the situation might have been different. She might not have been . . . I don't know . . . quite as troubled."

If Felicie read and tried to reason her way through what had happened to Renée and Stella, what did the other siblings do? "Sara did nothing *but* talk. Everything that we did manage to tell her she went around repeating: 'My sisters, you know, they survived Auschwitz, *this* is what happened to them, and *that.*' She didn't do this out of any malevolence, I think it was just her way of trying to come to terms with our experience." Selma and Morris, by contrast, became emotional every time the subject came up, but their curiosity remained limited, even clumsy: "It's hard to know what questions to ask when you don't know where to begin." Stella didn't see Victor again for more than ten years, until after he'd moved to Bologna, and by then he was more guarded than ever about his feelings.

As for Renée, she was internal and private. Later in life Stella found herself recounting experiences to Renée's sons that Renée never had herself, yet between the two sisters there remained, inevitably, an understanding—a vocabulary—that no one else shared. All one of them had to say was "Magda" or "Canada" or "potato." "Even today, after all these years, when I reflect on that march to Allach, and how she wouldn't let me give up, I think *this* is my sister. *This* is Renée."

In Los Angeles Stella, for a time, found a job with two Hungarian antiquarians; Renée, in a factory sewing clothes—more sewing. (When Stella tells me this, I think about Renée, at fifteen, beginning to sew her trousseau.) "It wasn't the future my sister had expected in Rhodes," Stella says dryly, "but between Rhodes and Los Angeles there came Auschwitz."

In the evenings they took English lessons; they needed a new language for this new life in a new world.

At one point Felicie had heard about an apartment on Beverly Drive and floated the idea that the three sisters consider living together. Stella and Renée went to check it out and in their imperfect English managed to ask the landlady if the neighborhood was safe. "Absolutely," she answered. "We never rent to people with cats or dogs, or to Jews."

The sisters looked at each other and then in mutual silent agreement came up with a different plan.

Renée went to try out Northern California, where Sara lived in Berkeley and where Felicie herself eventually moved, while Stella stayed behind, less and less enchanted with the city of the angels. "After Florence?

Can you imagine? To see a movie in French or Italian or go to a bookstore you had to take a tram all the way to Westwood. It was hard to meet people with similar interests. I thought of myself as that *povera donna sola abbandonata in questo popoloso deserto che appellano Los Angeles.* As in *La traviata*—you know."

"Um, Stella," I say, "wasn't that Paris Violetta was singing about?"

Stella laughs. "The *popoloso deserto* part was right—you can trust me on that."

Renée was no happier in Berkeley. She and Stella conferred and decided that they should return to Italy. It was where they were destined to be, surely. And after all Luigi was waiting; it was time.

83

Early in 1948 Renée and Stella traveled to New York in preparation for their return to Florence, and one of the first people they went to see was Fanny Levi, who did not hold back from expressing herself with regard to their intentions.

"*Ma siete matte?*"—are you out of your minds? "Italy is in ruins. It will take years, decades maybe, for the country to come back to itself. Italy's not the future—the future is America."

"But we didn't like California," Stella told her.

"Who goes to California? Not people like you. The place for people like you to build a life is New York City. Every kind of person is here, every possibility. This is where the two of you belong."

In a single flash of understanding, Renée and Stella realized that Fanny was right.

Well, likely right: "To be honest," Stella tells me, "not for the first time in these years, I acted on a feeling, an impulse. In the moment, it made sense. And yet I had no vision for myself. Not then or, really, ever."

• • •

She wrote to Luigi. It was one of the most difficult letters she had ever composed.

Sometime later, she tells me, leaping ahead to complete the story, Luigi became friends with her brother Victor, helping him to move to Italy after he left Congo, so she and Luigi stayed in each other's orbit, if not quite in each other's later lives. It was a long time, years, before she and Luigi met again, face-to-face. He was married by then and had a family. When they were alone he said to her, "By not coming back to Florence to marry me, Stella, you caused me the greatest pain I have ever experienced."

This was not easy to hear: "To this day I live with it as a *colpa*." *Colpa*: "fault," or "guilt." For following her own inclinations, or intuition; for knowing, or trying to know, her own mind and heart. "Wasn't it better not to have entered into a marriage that would have turned out to be wrong? If I'd married Luigi and then left, what kind of pain would *that* have caused?"

Several years after that, when still more time had passed, bringing, Stella hoped, an easing distance, she saw Luigi again in person. She went to embrace him, but he pulled back. "I was trying to find a way to thank him for all he had given me, and he had given me a great deal, but he was still expressing his hurt. I thought it was . . . disappointing." At Stella's end there was *un vero affetto*, true feeling, but at Luigi's, it seemed, bitterness had calcified.

"Is it possible that he was still in love with you?"

"I think it was more that he was in love with the idea of me. The actual me, by then, he couldn't know."

Stella's early years in New York were characterized by grit. She had the grit, and courage, to set Luigi, and herself, free. She had the grit, and discipline, to try to master English. She had the grit, and determination, to figure out how to take care of herself.

To find work Stella turned, logically, to members of the community in exile (only is it still exile, I wonder, when the place you come from no longer exists?). She started with two brothers, Hillel and Hertzel Franco, who had lived near the Levis in the Juderia and had come to New York before the war—Hillel (like Stella's brother Morris) even before she had a chance to meet him. As soon as the Francos heard that the two young women from Rhodes intended to settle in the city, they immediately invited them to dinner at their apartment on the Upper West Side, an evening at which other Rhodeslis were present too, among them Stella's neighbors, the Turiels. The Francos had an established import-export business, and they found a job for Stella that made good use of her facility with language, since many of their dealings were with the Belgian Congo and therefore conducted in French. Renée, meanwhile, went to work in the administrative offices of Saks.

The Francos exported American-made products that ranged from automotive tires to textiles; working with them gave Stella knowledge that would become consequential in her long professional life. Through Fanny, Stella eventually met another importer-exporter, an Italian man named Baldi who imported used clothes and textiles to Italy; his largely Puerto Rican staff required Stella to use her Spanish in addition to her Italian. After Baldi, Stella went into business for herself as an independent agent, helping Italian clients source American-made textiles (sheets, towels, remnants, and the like) for the Italian market, where in the postwar years there was a great need. Her work frequently took her to the South and into milieus that were traditional and dominated by men, but her acumen for figures and the ease with which she moved among different cultures and languages provided her with a handsome income for many years and connected her to a wide array of people and places. With characteristic Stella restlessness, though, and self-analysis, she looks back on the experience with mixed feelings.

"I worked hard and honestly, and I earned well," she tells me. "But the truth is that I'm ashamed and full of regret, because I dreamt of doing something else, of living an intellectual life. I tried, as you know, to study writing, then psychology, but I didn't succeed, either because I didn't have what it took, or I lacked the drive. To do these things you have to make sacrifices, more than I was up for at the time. The textile business came to me easily, it was like a gift."

For years, she goes on to tell me, she had her values all mixed up. In the early period in New York, she fell back into the familiarity with and apparent safety of this community of displaced Rhodeslis. She again mentions how she put too much energy into thinking about how she dressed, how she looked. Now, she says, she wishes she had directed that energy into going to school, and *staying* in school. To applying herself. To focusing herself.

As I listen to Stella, I find myself thinking of the young girl with the suitcase, ready for university in Italy; and then the older girl kicked out of school; the still older one facing, and failing, to take her graduating exams. And all this came before the camps. Carefully I ask Stella if she thinks that these obstacles, or disappointments, might explain how the rest of her life unfolded.

"It's possible," she says ruminatively. "But when I do some self-examining," she tells me ("self-examining" she says in English), "I realize that I believed everything should come to me by itself, without work or effort. But life is not like that. You have to say to your daughter, to any young person you care for: if you want to arrive at the point of doing something well—expertly—you have to put all of yourself into it. Cooking, dancing, studying, writing—it doesn't matter what. I see that now, I feel it in my body, what I didn't have then: discipline. Discipline is *the* thing."

84

New York wasn't working out for Renée; she didn't feel at ease in the big city. In 1949 she decided to return to California, where she found a job, married, had children, divorced—in short, found, and followed, her future.

After everything they'd been through together, Stella was bereft but remained convinced that, as Fanny Levi had predicted, New York was the city for her.

Completely on her own for the first time in her life, Stella moved to the Upper West Side, sharing an apartment with a friend named Willia in a building nicknamed il Vaticano. Why the Vatican? "Because no Jews lived in the actual Vatican, and during the war no Jews had been sheltered by the Vatican, but so many of them, and so many of them Italian, lived in this one building on the Upper West Side," Stella explains. "The term was ironic, of course."

It was in il Vaticano that, in the early fifties, Stella sat down at dinner one evening next to Paul Grundberg, whom she describes as one of the finest men she ever met and the first one she felt was "interested in me for me." Actually she met his parents first, at another of Willia's dinners, and was already captivated by the family story, with its own recent odyssey that included Turkey, where both of Paul's parents were born into German-Jewish families; Italy, where Paul himself was born and grew up in Milan and where his father, Sigmund, owned a thriving textile mill until 1938; Switzerland, where they moved next, having presciently parked some capital there; France, where they bought a house in Nice until it became untenable to continue living *there*; Portugal, which offered brief safe harbor, as it did to many Jews in transit in those years; and finally New York, where the family landed in 1940. These involuntary peregrinations left a bitter taste in Paul, who remained allergic to Italy, and much of Europe, for much of his life. He simply could not come to terms, Stella says, with the notion of a group of people who had contributed to the economy and culture, the life and lifeblood of a country, being tossed out summarily from one day to the next simply because of their religion.

That evening at il Vaticano Stella and Paul fell into conversation, and he offered to show her around Greenwich Village, where he lived. Their first date was a hot dog and coffee from Nedick's, on 8th Street and Sixth Avenue. "*Très elegant*," Stella says affectionately.

Paul, she quickly realized, was *molto retto*—upstanding, honest. A recent graduate in architecture from Columbia, he was working for a more established practitioner and happy to take on any project, no matter how modest. In Milan a chauffeur delivered Paul to school, but he never mentioned this to Stella; she heard it from his sister, Lotte, who spoke longingly, and often, about their lost luxury, not just the chauffeur but the cook, the nanny, the housemaid. Paul, instead, turned his back on all that, the same way he turned his back on Europe. He never gave himself airs. He cared about ideas, people, work.

After Stella sketches Paul's background and character and the beginnings of their courtship, she says to me, "I've said to you before that when I speak about the young woman in Rhodes, she sometimes feels like a different person to me, a character from a story, another world. This is also true of the Stella who married Paul. To this day I don't entirely understand her."

When my note-taking catches up, Stella explains further that Paul was a very fine person but that she didn't lose her head for him. A cousin of hers once said to her that she would never lose her head for anyone, and she has come to wonder whether he was correct. In Paul's case the love she felt for him was based on affection and respect. Beyond that she felt frivolous in comparison with him, not serious enough or sufficiently cultivated. "And I thought I might harm him."

I look up. Stella's face has hardened.

"Harm?" I ask.

She nods.

"Does that have something to do with what you'd lived through?" I ask.

"It never entered into my thinking. But, you know, many things didn't enter into my thinking at the time."

She goes on to say that by "harm," possibly what she really means is hold him back. She says that, for example, when Paul's educated friends came to dinner she could not easily contribute to the conversation, and before she knew it she was seeking refuge in the kitchen, dealing with the mechanics of the food and drink and so on, and when she had a whiff of that conventional domesticity—as she had, she has come to understand, in Florence, in conversations with Noferini during which they talked about their future together—she felt the first stirrings of a kind of suffocation that made her feel deeply, profoundly uneasy, almost unwell. As was characteristic of this time in her life, though, Stella was seized by feelings without quite understanding them or noted her thoughts without formulating them into a clear awareness of herself.

"I believe it says something that my husband and I were never able to make a home, or build a world, together," she goes on to tell me. "And what's more, Paul was perceptive. He knew that I was struggling. He knew that, after losing my home in Rhodes, I could not easily make one elsewhere. He and I went from house to house, rooms to rooms, borrowed places from friends and family that were always temporary. We weren't rooted because I was unable to put down roots, either because I wasn't ready to, or didn't want to. And yet he deserved more."

Not for the first time Stella tells me that she wasn't made for marriage: "I felt this way about marriage early on in Rhodes, and it became very clear to me once I was married myself. I needed to be free in life. I needed to be on my own in order to breathe."

85

The following Saturday, as if coming at this part of her life from a different but obviously related angle, Stella tells me that when she left the camps she didn't have her period for a very long time. It resumed, briefly, during the year she was living in Italy, and then it stopped again. Her cousin Sara never again had a period. Renée did; she ended up having two children.

When Stella returned to New York she went to see a gynecologist, a Dr. Wimpfheimer, who performed a minor procedure on her and reassured her that her period would return, which it soon did.

Life took her forward. She met and married Paul, and she became pregnant. On December 6, 1954, she gave birth to a son, John. Afterward a beaming Dr. Wimpfheimer came to see her and said, "You remember you told me that you didn't think you'd ever have a child?"

With great joy, and relief, Stella was able to tell him that he had been right and she wrong.

.   .   .

After Stella and Paul separated three years later, she came to another difficult realization: she'd understood clearly that she wasn't ready to be a
wife, and as much as she adored her son, she saw that she wasn't ready
to be a single mother either. "I didn't have what it took. I was afraid and
I was alone. I had no family here. No sisters, no aunts, no mother, no
community. I suppose you could say that I was lost . . ."

She went to see a psychiatrist for the first time when she was a new,
struggling mother. She was very clear about not wanting to find the answer
in the camps; she wanted to find the answer in herself. Other people who
had come out of that place, that experience, had married and had children,
and seemed to do both successfully. Why, she wanted to know, couldn't she?

"That was my thinking at the time," Stella tells me. "Though it's
true, I see now, that I never assimilated that experience, or digested it.
I didn't want to, or I wasn't able to. If one of these analysts I'd seen had
been *bravo*, truly *bravo*, maybe then, maybe he, or she, could have helped
me through this understanding; even if it hurt me, or troubled me, I
would have resolved certain things. Because starting, in fact, with the
racial laws—I've said this to you before—I became cut off from myself,
from my path. Isolated. And then . . . then the camps. All these actions
against the Jews gave me a fear of making bonds. These ruptures in my
life were"—she searches for the word—"consequential."

She adds that in certain states of mind, though, she's not sure it's
right, necessarily, to blame the professionals she saw. They were skilled
and well-intentioned; it was possible that she wasn't ready, yet, to receive
what they had to offer. She was obstinate, resistant, skeptical, tough. "It
may surprise you, but I am not always the easiest person."

Stella takes a deep slow breath then closes down the subject of her
mothering by saying that these are not easy memories to revisit. She explains that when John was nine, one of her analysts, a woman as it hap-
pens, proposed that she send him to a progressive boarding school in
Scotland, and she unwisely, as she now thinks, followed the psychiatrist's
advice. When I ask Stella if he wanted to go, she answers sharply, "What
child wants to leave his mother?"

John stuck it out in Scotland for two years. When he returned he spent summers with Stella but the rest of the year with his father, who had remarried and moved to Chatham in upstate New York: "I think that was best for him," Stella says. "I hope it was."

Stella's eyes go quite faraway here. It's clear how difficult this conversation is for her to have; and yet she seems, at the same time, determined to have it, determined to put, to try to put, this experience too into words. Some words.

Eventually I ask her if she has had this talk, or a talk like this, with her son. She answers that she's tried. And that she's not sure she's succeeded. "I did once say to him that I may not have been a great mother, but I did, at least, choose him a perfect father."

86

After her marriage ended, Stella's life was not without intimate relationships, but her most significant and enduring human connections were her friendships.

As we sit together in her apartment this winter Saturday, with Stella, approaching ninety-eight, in the winter of her life, she speaks to me about some of these friends of hers, so many of them gone now, and I can feel the ghosts gathering. Estelle Pilot, for example: A copywriter Stella met through Fanny Levi, Estelle was born in Bangor, Maine, into one of two Jewish families in town. Growing up, she was once asked by a schoolmate where her horns were; "I left them at home," she answered tartly. After Estelle had moved to New York her mother would phone her on a Saturday and wonder what she was up to. "Reading the Bible" was her answer. "But you're not religious." "What does the Bible have to do with being religious?" In her old age, when she lived on Bleecker Street, Estelle would go downstairs to let her dog out for a walk on his own; then she would return to her apartment, lean out the window, and wait for him to return. "Sir, Lady," she would call down to a passer-by when he did, "I'm going to buzz open the front door, can you let my dog in?"

Estelle was a character, and Stella loves characters. She was an American Felicie: she read everything, knew everything; she had a fierce intelligence. So too did the "women from Brandeis" that Stella met through Ellen Levine, a writer she was introduced to through Fanny Levi's son Leone and his wife, Chris. Stella, Leone, and Chris rented a series of summer shares in the Hamptons whose various bedrooms they filled up by putting ads in the newspaper and interviewing possible candidates. Stella brought John; one of the housemates brought dogs that disrupted the peace of their grumpy neighbor Willem de Kooning. She became friendly with the artists Costantino Nivola and Gert Berliner, who'd been sent to Sweden on a Kindertransport. Both in the Hamptons and back in the city she joined a serious poker game with Woody Allen and the playwrights Arthur Kopit and Jack Gelber where they didn't break for dinner until eleven or even midnight and where she became known as the woman who separated all these savvy men from their money. "It was the best of New York, New York at its best," Stella says. "I met so many interesting people in those years. I was fortunate. If you are open to it, life is full of different vivid characters, a theater of personalities."

Many, many people have come and gone in her life, Stella continues. She puts this sentence in the past tense, but not a single Saturday goes by that our conversations aren't interrupted by a phone call (or two, or more) from Stella's friends or relatives, who remain in touch with her these days largely by telephone. I have never known anyone of her age, or even roughly approaching her age, who has as populated, connected—interconnected—a world as Stella does. And yet at the same time I can see, in each individual day, how alone, and lonely, she often feels.

Stella is well aware that her postwar life could easily have taken her in other, more conventional directions. Most of the young women she knew in Rhodes, both those who left before the deportation and those who survived the camps, married within the community, but Stella had no interest in re-creating the world she had grown up in in this way. She's still not sure where these feelings originated, whether they began far back, under the unspoken influence of her mother's fate—a Notrica who had married down—or whether they were wrapped up in her romantic life ("I did things that I could never tell my siblings, except maybe Sara"), or her interrupted education, or the fact that as a single woman she had to earn her own living. However she got there, Stella was an outsider, and while being an outsider caused her moments of considerable difficulty in her life, she has come to value the freedom it conferred on her over time.

"I do believe that as we travel through life we become a different person in every situation, or context, or phase," she says. "What I find myself asking now is: What remains, what is consistent, in an individual person? In my own case what I see as a theme is a gradual opening up. This, in the end, is what America gave me: an immense opening up, finally. I don't think I would have been able to lead the same life in Italy, which after the war was still very closed and classist, with thinking that could be quite restrictive, especially with regard to how a woman should conduct herself. Certainly, if the Juderia had continued to exist, I wouldn't have belonged there. In New York I was financially independent, I could be free to move though different circles, I was not limited. And I never wanted to be limited."

87

As Stella aged, her friends became more central in her life than her siblings, though inevitably her brothers and in particular her sisters remained a key link to the Juderia. Of all of them Selma, who in Stella's early childhood had been like a second mother to her, encapsulated and expressed that lost world of the Juderia the most powerfully, in part because she was the only of the siblings to observe, all through the year, the holidays and rituals— she was the only of them who remained at all religious—and in part because of how she organized her household, devoting Thursday and Friday, just as their mother had, to preparing for Shabbat, which she celebrated most every week. As the oldest of the girls, Selma had seen and learned firsthand, from Miriam and their aunts and grandmothers, how to make *burekas* and *boyus*, *pastels* and *pastelikus*, and all the other variously shaped and differently filled savory pastries that were the staple of nearly every household in the Juderia, and she was an expert baker as well, producing a steady stream of *baklava*, *travados*, *kurabiyes*—more varied shapes. She made marzipan too, and cakes (sponge, clementine, lemon), meringues, puddings, fruit pastes, candies, and candied fruit, so that to step into her kitchen or sit down at her table was to be engulfed with scents and flavors that were of a commanding Proustian intensity, and whenever Stella visited she cherished them as among the most assiduous but also some of the most fragile threads that continued to connect her to her childhood and youth.

Selma and Sara lived to be very old, ninety-nine and ninety-eight respectively, and wound down their lives in California, as did Morris, Felicie, and Renée. Of all the Levi children only Victor remained in Europe, in Bologna. To the end, Stella was closest to Renée—"How not, after all we had lived through together?"—flying out to Northern California whenever she was needed, or wanted, or could.

"And now," Stella tells me, "the baby of the family is the oldest one alive—the *only* one alive."

Playing across Stella's lined but so-vivid face, as she says this, I see a mini movie of her younger self, drawn from the family photographs that her older siblings took with them when they left Rhodes and that came back to her later in life, images that she and I have looked at together many times over the years: Stella and her siblings standing outside the city walls, or sitting in front of their *cabina* on the beach, or posing in front of the sukkah they built in their courtyard, or walking out to Rodino on a Saturday afternoon. In all of these photographs she is always the smallest, the youngest, the last in line.

"There's an old adage," I tell her. "I wonder if you've heard it. The youngest child is the one who gets to tell the story—the one who gets to have the last word. I think it was Henry James who said something like that."

"Having the last word," she says, "can be very lonely."

88

Stella's life, like all long lives, has been lived in chapters. One of the most important began about twenty years ago when she was sliding toward eighty, an age at which most people begin to turn inward, do less in the world, and need less from it. Stella instead did more and needed more. She began to volunteer at the Sephardic House, which morphed into the American Sephardic Federation when it moved into a building on 16th Street, sharing space with the Center for Jewish History, among other organizations. In the lobby one day she was introduced to Natalia Indrimi, who would soon establish the Centro Primo Levi with Alessandro Di Rocco, a world-renowned neurologist from Genoa; eight years later they would be joined by Alessandro Cassin, whose grandfather Stella had met after the war at the Pensione Annalena. Each, in different ways, would become central figures in Stella's later years.

Stella approaches her understanding of friendship, as she has much in her life, by discarding any preconceptions about what such a connection might be, how it might look or unfold. With Natalia, for example, she says, "It was an immediate, extraordinary thing, this connection of ours. It happened on so many levels, intellectual, psychological, emotional." She and Natalia are not from the same generation. They are not mother and daughter or two sisters or cousins, relationships, obviously, that Stella has known well, and lived deeply; but their bond has evolved into one of great significance. "Very delicately Natalia has helped me to see, finally, who I am. I think that if you are a sensitive person, an awake person, this is what can happen to you in life. You have to be courageous, though, because friendship requires vulnerability; it too is a leap of faith, a risk."

With Alessandro Cassin, Stella has found an intimate male friend unlike any other in her long life. Over weekly Shabbat dinners he has accompanied her on an extended journey into her past while engaging with her intellectually, studying ancient Hebrew with her, and joining her in singing old Sephardic songs that he has helped draw out of that capacious memory of hers. Like Natalia, Alessandro has found in Stella, in her life, in her thinking, qualities that she was not always aware of. Because they valued her in new ways, she has come to value herself in some of these ways too: not just for what she lived, and endured, but how she has come to interpret and think about what she lived and endured.

These vibrant connections have brought unanticipated meaning to the phase of life that in Italian is sometimes called *la terza età*, literally, and to my ear quite beautifully, "the third age." I don't think it's correct to say that this period of Stella's life has made up for the deprivations that she experienced in the earlier parts, but there is no question that hers has been an unusually rich, textured, and evolving old age, one in which she has drawn many people into her orbit—me among them—and given to, and taken from, each of us, each in differently unforgettable ways.

89

There is another friend Stella wants to talk to me about: Öcsi Ullmann—"He was like a brother to me." It was Öcsi who, in 1977, helped Stella over a great hurdle in her life by insisting that she return to Rhodes, thirty-three years after she had left the island.

Öcsi and his brother were born to a Hungarian Jewish father and a Greek mother; the couple married in Turkey, where the boys grew up before moving to London. His Turkish "blood"—and Stella's—made them fast friends: "You're from Rhodes? You have Turkish ancestors? We're related then," he announced the first time they met.

Öcsi ran a gallery that specialized in rugs and tapestries in atmospheric rooms above Madison Avenue and later on the Upper West Side. Ebullient, opinionated, and expansive, he traveled everywhere and seemed to know everything; if he trusted you, he always said what he was thinking, without editing. "When he heard that I hadn't yet faced returning to Rhodes he said, 'That's impossible. You must, it's something that has to happen'—and he singlehandedly made it happen."

Stella had been resisting; she had been afraid. She would never have gone, at least not then, without this push. Almost without realizing it, there she was, in the spring of 1977: she, Öcsi, and Öcsi's then boyfriend flying to Athens, then to Rhodes. When she stepped off the plane, she was trembling.

The airport was near Trianda, and instantly the feelings came pouring back: the many weekends they'd spent there with their Greek friends the Papathanasises, their retreat there after the bombings.

The taxi dropped them at a hotel in the modern part of town. They went to the Juderia on foot.

"There are not even words," Stella says as her eyes darken. "I cannot speak about this, not now."

As I look at her I think of a line in Proust in which he describes Saint-Loup's girlfriend Rachel, the actress, as having her personality concentrated in her eyes. That is how Stella strikes me, in this moment.

We break here for the day.

90

The following week Stella has found the words, some of them, after all:

"I'll tell you what it was like. It was like carrying in my stomach an enormous weight—a cancer, an ulcer, only it wasn't either. It was the fear: the fear of returning, the fear of finding—no, of not finding. The fear of finding everything gone. Everything *was* gone. Everything that mattered."

Stella felt like a foreigner in her home: her one-time home. Then as they crossed the piazza, the Kay Ancha, Öcsi, who spoke Greek, heard a young man whisper to a friend, "I know her." He told Stella, who turned around and after hesitating for a beat identified the speaker: Isaac (Izzy) Alhadeff, whose mother had been born in Beirut under the Ottomans and therefore was among the Turkish citizens who were spared deportation.

It was her Argos moment, though instead of being recognized by a dog, she was recognized by a boy—a boy now grown into a man.

Izzy Alhadeff was the first human connection to the Juderia Stella experienced on this return, but others would follow. She went to see the Soriano family who, also being Turkish, had similarly been spared deportation and had moved for a time to Turkey; they were among the first members of the community to come back after the war and were among the even fewer who chose to remain in Rhodes. She went to see Mihali Papathanasis, who had opened a travel agency: "I don't think we stopped crying for half an hour, at least."

When they did, Mihali asked her about Renée. She wasn't ready yet to come back, Stella told him. But someday maybe.

Öcsi and Stella went to see the synagogue, the Kahal Shalom; it was broken and empty, not restored, as it would be later. They went by her house, her friends' houses. All the doors were shut, whereas in Stella's time, in her Juderia, during the day her mother left their kitchen door open, as did Ermana Rifka Cohen and Ermana Behora Soriano and Ermana Dalva, of course—the blurred demarcation between house and street, private and public, extending further the feeling of at-homeness that a small child had nearly everywhere she roamed in the neighborhood.

They walked by the bakery and the ruins of the Kahal Grande, the larger synagogue, which had been bombed. The neighborhood still, after all these years, showed the scars of war. Three decades later, pieces of broken, toppled walls were lying where they fell; houses stood without roofs, thresholds without doors, windows without glass. Weeds had sprung up, gardens withered.

Could it still be called the Juderia if, essentially, no Jews lived there any longer?

91

After the first trip others followed, and they continued all the way up to 2015, when I met Stella in Rhodes. Maybe this was how it had to happen: in regular microdoses, like a series of inoculations, with the grief, the loss, the sense of dislocation, and the pain spread out over time and in the company of different configurations of people. In this way Stella faced, but as was clear to me when I was there, perhaps didn't entirely vanquish—as how could she?—the demon of return.

Little by little she began to add Rhodes to the points on her compass. She became more at ease, more *courageous*—this is the word she uses. When she went to Italy for work, she would make a quick visit. She traveled there on a tour with members of the Broome Street synagogue. Her cousin Sara came from Cape Town. She arranged a rendezvous with Rhodeslis from Brussels, where scores of them had moved after 1960, when the Belgian Congo became independent. They stayed in modern hotels, gathered around tables to drink and eat, to reminisce. They cried so much the makeup washed off their faces. But also they laughed: "Yes, laughter was possible—necessary in fact."

These returning Rhodeslis gave a place, something of a place, to the people who had disappeared. *Remember the* capitano *and how he courted the girl with the grippe—* Or: *Leon Cohen, the shoemaker's son, who was just learning the trade, he had feelings for Renée, he was younger than she was by four or five years, he blushed and his hand trembled when he went to measure her foot—* Or: *Giuseppe Hazan, Yosefacci, the boy who lived with his older siblings because his parents kept a shop on Halki* e andava a fare il peripatetico con Frate Angelino, *the last time I saw him in the street, he was carrying* The Sorrows of Young Werther *under his arm, and I mocked him for reading such a lofty book—*

The girl with the grippe, the besotted son of the *calzolaio*, Goethe-reading Yosefacci: they were all incinerated in the ovens of Auschwitz. Where else, and by who else, would they ever be remembered?

92

In 1995 Stella finally persuaded Renée to return to Rhodes. Renée had been adamant. Up to that point she had been like Lucia Franco, who never went back, or Clara Gabriel, whom Stella went to see in Brussels, hoping to convince her. Clara's response: "I will never set foot on that piece of earth again."

With Renée Stella tried harder. She tried until she prevailed. With Renée, maybe because Sara Notrica joined them, maybe because they were all three together, the memories were tidal: They went to the beach, they spoke about the diving board, the *cabina*, the *gelati* they bought from Rosetti; they visited Monte Smith; they went by the school of the *suore*, the *aeronautica* where they had been confined. They walked along all the streets of the Juderia, block by block, building by building. Nobody, though, wanted to knock on the door of the Levi house, where they heard a Greek man lived, married to a Russian woman; nobody could face going inside.

Stella took Renée to see the Papathanasises. Mihali wasn't there, and they asked his daughter not to tell him they had come by. They wanted to surprise him.

Renée was the great friend of Mihali's youth, the woman he had offered (implausibly but generously) to marry, to save her from being deported, just as his brother, Yoti, had made the same offer to Stella. The surprise nearly killed him. When he saw her his face simply liquefied.

In Soroni, Sara, who spoke Greek because she'd grown up with a Greek housekeeper, was able to do some asking around in the village, in an attempt to find out what had happened to Miriam's friend Mihali Elias; finally they found a neighbor who was able to tell them that he had died some years earlier. One of his daughters lived nearby, though, the fellow added, in a village called Kalavarda. Onward the trio drove. Sara did some more asking around and was directed to a house, where Renée and Stella found the young girl they had known; she was grown now and a mother, but recognizable in an instant. "She looked at us as if we were ghosts," Stella says, "which in a way I suppose we were."

Renée visited only that once. Stella kept going. Over the years she saw the Juderia, what had been the Juderia, fill up with shops hawking T-shirts and souvenirs. She watched tourists sip their sodas and bubbly water as they sat at the foot of a black slab put up in the piazza in 2002 to memorialize—in Greek, Hebrew, English, French, Italian, and Judeo-Spanish—the Jewish victims of Rhodes and Kos. These travelers came for the beach, the ruins perhaps, and to shop; they were unaware of what this neighborhood had once been, what it had once meant.

Eventually Stella helped plan the restoration of the Kahal Shalom and contributed to a museum established by her younger cousin Aron Hasson in what had been the women's prayer rooms attached to the sanctuary. After the museum opened in 1997, Selma's daughter Esther donated one of the special dresses that Miriam had bought from an itinerant Turkish vendor over the years and had sent to the States with the older girls when they left. These dresses—Sara donated a similar one to a museum in Berkeley, where she lived—were made out of velvet and embroidered with gold or silver thread. Miriam didn't wear these garments but instead collected them for their rarity and craftsmanship; the older girls might put them on but only once a year, for Purim, and only if they promised to be very careful.

The dress, along with a number of objects contributed by other families, returned to Rhodes, but for the majority of people who bought, kept, or collected these things, the only trace of them that remains in the Juderia is their name: in 2009 a metal and plexiglass structure in the shape of a large book was installed in the courtyard of the synagogue, its leaves printed with the names of the Jews of Rhodes, every single name of every single person known to have been gathered up and loaded onto those three boats on July 23, 1944.

Before I left Rhodes that summer I visited, Stella took me to see this large book. With effort she turned its heavy leaves for me, reading one name after another, the names of her family, the names of her friends, the names of the dead. It had been years—nearly seven decades, I realized as I stood there—since most of these names had been said aloud in the Juderia.

93

I have been saving up some questions.

If there'd been no war, no deportation, no camps, I ask Stella the following Saturday, can she imagine what her feelings about Rhodes would have been?

An inappropriate thing to ask? I can't tell at first from Stella's face. All I can tell is that she's thinking. I've seen her think like this many times before, retreat into silence or a pause. The intensity with which she turns inward reminds me of something Hannah Arendt once asked herself: Where are we when we think? Arendt found her way toward an answer by reflecting on a parable by Kafka, where he imagined a battleground on which the forces of the past and the future clash with each other.

After a moment, several moments, she says, "It's unknowable, isn't it? Rhodes ended how it ended. It's not easy to imagine the alternate reality." But she goes on to try: "If there'd been no war," she says, "we would have left anyway."

"What makes you so sure?"

"Because there were no men to marry!"

She laughs. Then: "We had no future there. We were a community of the old and young women, mostly women. Time would have tugged us further forward to modernity, no matter what, and modernity would have been different, it would have changed everything, it would have opened up new paths, inevitably. If Renée and I had left, my parents would have been alone, and we could never have left them alone, so they would have come with us, likely at first to Los Angeles."

And what would her father, her mother have done in Los Angeles?

"They would have adapted," Stella says. "What else? That's what we Jews have always done. I've said that to you before, have I not?"

I wonder, again, about her anger: Whether she feels it, what she does about it if she does?

She thinks for a moment. "I am a person who easily gets angry about small things . . . but for this thing, the biggest thing, I don't feel anger. I have questions of my own instead. I would like to understand better, the origin of all this antisemitism that goes back thousands of years. As I often say, there are genocides of other people, there is the way African Americans were treated in this country, and continue to be treated. Hatred seems hardwired into us as human beings. But this thing with the Jews, with the war, it is so perplexing. It was perpetrated by a people who were more cultivated, literary, educated than anyone else in Europe. You saw it in their music, their philosophy—I am not the first person to reason along these lines, to mention that the Germans were the people of Bach and Mendelssohn and Goethe and so on. I mean, you saw it even in their uniforms. When we stepped off the trains and saw the SS, they were dressed immaculately. They dressed immaculately to annihilate human beings."

Of course, Stella goes on to say, it would never have happened if the rest of the people of Europe, even those who didn't want the war, hadn't turned away, and that includes the Italians, who were far more complicit than is commonly understood or discussed. This is one of those conversations, Stella believes, that has not yet been had fully enough: "Not nearly."

And then there is the absurdity of what happened in Rhodes specifically: "I've said it to you before, and I probably will again. I still ask myself: Why? Why did they care about such a small community, to come so far and nearly at the last minute, two months before Greece was liberated, to do what? Deport, basically, the old. What was the point of rounding up 1,650 human beings, taking them on a voyage that lasts a month, and costs, who knows what? Couldn't they have better used the money for arms to defend themselves?"

After a moment Stella wonders whether it is possible to hate to this degree. It's what she wonders most, she tells me, about the human soul. "Sometimes I speculate that this thing was no longer about a hatred of the Jews, even. The Germans had built a machine and kept using it, even though they knew the war was over."

She pauses for a moment, returns to, as I imagine it, that battleground of thought Kafka described.

"For me personally, as for so many of us, it was a traumatic experience. But to have destroyed a community in that manner? There will never be Jews anymore in Rhodes. Never. They succeeded in separating a people from their place, forever.

"I ask myself why, but there is no answer. You do not find a reason. You tell the story, as I have done to you. It's all that you can do."

94

You tell the story. But why did Stella wait so long? Why did she wait until she was well into her nineties before sitting down and talking about, properly talking about, what happened to her and her family?

She begins by reminding me: she *did* speak about Rhodes. She agreed to appear in two documentaries, Rebecca Samonà's *L'isola delle Rose* and Ruggero Gabbai's *The Longest Journey*. Her son knew what happened to her, in broad strokes. Her granddaughter interviewed her for a school project, and naturally she spoke about her experience with her friends, her close friends, over the years. She was not one of those survivors who closes that particular door and never so much as cracks it open again; but nor was she interested in becoming a storyteller of the Holocaust, she reminds me, someone who tells the same stories over and over, even as the storyteller changes and her memories change.

"I didn't want my identity to be fixed in that way. I didn't want that number tattooed on my arm. I didn't want them to look at me and gasp, '*Poverina.*' I didn't want to be a victim."

Stella goes on to add that there were plenty of people who had already told their stories well, besides, notably for her, Primo Levi himself. And there was a personal reason why she resisted telling her story. She heard a critical voice in her mind—largely her *own* critical voice, she sees that now—asking who she thought she was, wondering by what authority she was to speak about the Juderia, about the life that happened there, and afterward. But her thinking has changed over the years, especially as she's grown older. "Many things come to you late in life," she tells me. "I've never said this before to anyone, but when you arrive at a certain age, you're no longer afraid of being ridiculous."

After a moment, with her eyes glimmering, she adds, "And then you came along and were curious. And patient with me, even though I wasn't always so . . . so easy. And in speaking to you I have learned a good deal about myself. As I tell you my stories, I learn. One thing I learn is that there is no single truth; there is a changing truth along that *cammin della nostra vita* and you understand a good deal from going back, returning, and more than once, to what you thought you knew, and felt, and believed.

"And in the end, you know, I trusted you."

I point out that it took her a while before she actually did.

"You have to earn trust, Michael, wouldn't you agree?"

The look she gives me now I might once have characterized as fierce. I no longer see it that way. I see it as the look of someone who is fully present, unafraid to speak her mind, unwilling to make difficult moments easy or palatable, and who is, above all, truthful, or as truthful as she can be given the way memory behaves and the mind evolves over time.

"I do agree," I say. "But I think also . . . also that it might require a leap of faith—on both sides."

Stella takes this in. "We both took that leap, I believe."

The silence that envelops us feels almost material, to be made of something tangible like cloth, like a large sail or a tent—a sail that has captured the wind that carried us on this journey, a tent that has defined and enclosed our time together, our many Saturdays over these many years.

"There's something else," Stella says after a moment.

"Oh?"

"Well, our talking, it seems like it's kept me alive."

95

What would you say, I ask Stella, if you could, to all the children who will be born after all the survivors have died and the Holocaust becomes an event preserved and recounted in books and documentaries and museums, something that happened *back then* to people whose eyes they can no longer look into, whose voices and stories they can no longer hear in person with their own ears? What would you want them to know?

Before Stella answers, I go on to add that I sometimes think of her, or nominate her, as the Last Survivor. Eventually there will be one: the Last Survivor who tells all. Not all; that's wrong. Who tells, as Stella has told me, the story of what she has lived and known, as authentically and truthfully as memory permits; and who has revisited her story at different points in her life; and who has continued all her life to think about what happened to her, and the possible reasons for it, and how it formed her. And who has, increasingly, felt the importance of sharing what she lived: The world she came from, with its reach so far back in time. The world she was thrust into. The world she eventually discovered, and built, for herself.

She ponders for a moment before answering, "I would say: do not hate another person. Why should you hate another person? Because he's mean, or because he comes from a different background than you do? Because his beliefs are different from yours?"

Then:

"I was born into a particular religion, as many of us are. For me, as a girl, ritual and belief were inseparable. I knew that Felicie wasn't religious, my brother smoked on Shabbat, and my mother said, 'Go where you want, do what you wish, as long as you're out of sight.' I myself grew up to be a nonbeliever. But the way we lived with the synagogue just in front of our home, and my father running there for every service, every prayer; and a mezuzah on the door; and on Shabbat, the meal, the kiddush . . . all those holidays, all those habits. What do I do with all this? Negate it, deny it? The traditions I grew up in made me who I am. And not only that. I have been formed by all the books I've read, I know that there is a long, long history behind the world I was born into. These little tribes that fought, took this land of Canaan, and built a temple. They devised the idea of a single God. Bit by bit they formed a religion. They learned from the Egyptians, they learned in Babylon. They grew, they developed, they became a people—well, at least that's the story.

"You don't need to believe to be a Jew. You are a Jew because you are born into a tradition. But whether you believe in God, it's important to remember a simple thing: no one idea about God is better than another. In the end we are all similar, everyone with differences and defects. What's essential is to value humanity."

96

More than once over the years I've said to Stella that she is one of the best models I've ever found of how to age with grace and grit, sometimes also with stubbornness: beginning to study ancient Hebrew in her mid-nineties, reading unceasingly, venturing out safely nearly every day, remaining in touch with the many friends she is connected to, not letting any of us get away with a vague or lazy thought or less-than-perfect behavior. But sometimes when I've said this to her I've perceived a hesitation, a silent disagreement, at her end, and slowly I've come to realize that by insisting on how impressively she was doing, I was in a way obscuring or negating, or anyway failing to leave room for, the bleak feelings she had about where she found herself at this stage of her life. And where she found herself, when she spoke about it candidly, was not often pleasant: she had this mind, this intact mind, that was underused, "squandered." The days sometimes blurred into trivial chores and tasks. She was lonely and tired. She felt she had outlived her purpose. "There are moments when I don't know if I can carry on." Or: "Think of Primo Levi. He knew when he had come to the end."

Primo Levi (despite their shared last name he and Stella are not related) has been an important touchstone for Stella for many years: a careful reader of human nature; precise in his thinking; angry as needed; a storyteller (of the most important stories); and the first person to write about his own experience of the camps that she, like many people, ever read. But I know that by bringing him up in this context she is thinking about the way he died in April 1987.

"Does it even matter if he was dizzy and fell down those stairs or chose to end his life?" she says, as if she is anticipating the question I am trying to figure out how to ask. "It's not how one dies that's important but how one lives."

I wait for a moment before saying, "Still you wonder, I wonder, did it have to do with—"

As often, she is ahead of me.

"It's what people ask. I've heard people say they believe he escaped the camps mentally, but what does that mean, 'escape'? My own mind . . . it won't let go. I still think about the train, I try to bring back the details. I know we put up a kind of curtain for my father, so that he could pee in privacy, some privacy, but I can't remember how we rigged it. I don't know how we survived the two weeks. How we understood what it meant when my uncle Notrica died, or *if* we understood, and his body was taken away in the same station where I washed my hair. I remember his death and I remember my courage, or stupidity, however you look at it, with Sara and Renée, the three of us, going to that pump, but I don't know how I even dared to ask.

"These two events happening at the same time and in the same place. What does it mean, any of it?

211

"And that's just the train ride. Then comes the year that followed. No, it's with me, I may think about it differently, but it's always asking me to go back, to look back . . ."

Surely, I suggest, it was always with Primo Levi too.

Stella considers for a moment before answering, "He had given that which he had to give. He didn't write anymore because he had written everything he had to say. He had gone to the schools to speak to the young. He had been interviewed many times. He had completed his work here. He was ready to go."

97

Each year on January 27, the anniversary of the day the Soviet Army entered and liberated Auschwitz, Centro Primo Levi observes International Holocaust Remembrance Day by participating in a ceremony known as the Reading of the Names: lecterns and microphones are set up in front of the Italian Consulate on Park Avenue, where, beginning at nine o'clock in the morning, people come and go over the next six or seven hours and take turns reading the names, last before first, of every single one of the ten thousand men, women, and children deported from Italy and Italian-controlled territories during the Fascist-Nazi persecution.

Despite the cold Stella infallibly makes the trip uptown. Sometimes she reads; sometimes she stands or sits in back, sipping tea and being greeted by, and talking to, the dozens of people who partake of this ritual. Sometimes the cold drives her inside, or home—but she always appears.

One year when it is my turn to stand at a lectern the pages open to the letter *L*: quite by chance, mysterious chance, it falls to me to read out the names of Stella's family. In years past when I have read I've always felt my eyes dart to the right side of the page, where a column contains certain pieces of information: when the man, or woman, or child was born, and where; who his or her spouse or parents were; where he or she was arrested and to where deported; and then one of two phrases, "*È sopravvissuto alla Shoah*" or "*Non è sopravvissuto alla Shoah*"—survived the Holocaust or did not. This is one year when my eyes don't look to the right, because after all the time I've spent listening to Stella I know by now what happened to these people, Stella's family, the Levis of Rhodes.

Knowing is remembering. Reading is remembering. Naming is remembering.

There are different ways to remember.

In the fall of 2019 Natalia Indrimi and Alessandro Cassin organized a monthlong pop-up exhibition in an old carriage house in the West Village to commemorate the story of the Jews of Rhodes that itself became, I think even to some degree surprising them, its own unexpected act of remembering.

They called it *Los Corassones Avlan*, after a phrase in Judeo-Spanish that was often used in the Juderia and has no real equivalent in English. *Los corassones*—or *korasones*—*avlan*: literally "hearts speak"—but it wasn't clear to me quite what that meant, or said, until Stella explained: "You're in your kitchen preparing dinner, or you're sitting in an armchair and reading a book. A friend pops into your head: you see her face, you think of a remark she made, a story she told. A moment later, there's a knock at your door. You open it, and there is that same friend. '*Ah*,' you say, '*los korasones avlan.*'"

Hearts speak? Hearts summon? Hearts know? For a month, in the West Village, hearts spoke about Rhodes, and summoned, and knew, the lost world of the Juderia. Natalia and Alessandro set up a display of textiles, a few pieces of silver, a pair of *takos*. They projected a series of photographs and film clips of old Rhodes onto bare brick walls. They served *burekas* made by Davide Roubini, a baker who spent weeks testing them out, then adjusting them to meet Stella's rigorous standards, which were made all the more rigorous for having to approximate the remembered flavors of nearly a century ago.

On some evenings a musician came to sing Sephardic songs. On others there were screenings of the documentary about the Juderia made by

Rebecca Samonà, the granddaughter of Victoria Sidis Licitri and Ernesto Licitri, who had turned to Stella for help understanding her family's unexplored past. On other evenings there were conversations, between Stella and her cousin Isabelle Levy; between Stella and her former neighbor, Elliot Turiel, the little boy she'd seen born (*"Ke paryo? Ijo!"*) who grew up to be a professor of psychology at Berkeley. I myself spoke to Stella one night about the grandmothers, mothers, and daughters of the Juderia.

For a whole month something greater than these various component parts took place, afternoon following afternoon, evening following evening, in a courtyard on West 4th Street, off a busy, undistinguished stretch of Sixth Avenue, where a flood of people, some having traveled from far away, came to pack the tiny rooms. They were the descendants of Rhodes, the children, grandchildren, nieces and nephews who grew up hearing stories about the Juderia and the people who lived there, who had been sung to sleep with old Judeo-Spanish lullabies, who had tasted the *burekas* and *pastelles* and *travados* whose recipes had passed down across the generations, who kept tucked in an old drawer photographs that needed identifying or an object that needed explaining, a filigreed bracelet or a textile embroidered a century ago that had long outlived the time and place in which it was made, traded, cherished, gifted, mended, used, and understood. They came for the music, the talks, the tea, and the approximated pastries . . . and they came for Stella, who sat like a village elder in a thrift-shop armchair draped in a faded Turkish kilim and listened to their stories and answered their questions and asked a number of her own.

I was present one evening when a woman, after patiently waiting her turn in line, asked Stella if she had known her mother, Fortunée. (She was a different Fortunée from the one who lit the candles and said the prayers at Auschwitz.) Stella looked momentarily perplexed, and then, *boom*: "You mean *Fortunata*—that's how we knew her in Rhodes. But of course: Fortunata Soriano. She was in my sister Renée's class and her mother, Behora Soriano, was my mother's great friend, they went for *passeggiate* together and to the movies and she and her husband used to stop at our house for havdalah after Shabbat . . ." Stella went on to connect the dots—where she lived, what she looked like as a girl—and then she produced a memory, which you could see from the way her face transformed, gradually, as if it were suddenly being lit from within, was new even to her: "Do you know," she said, "in Auschwitz your mother during roll call used to conceal her eyebrow tweezers in her *mouth*?"

Stella paused, then emitted a quiet, wry, many-layered laugh. "I saw her take them out myself. She said, 'I have such heavy eyebrows, you know, and it's the safest place to hide them. We're not allowed to speak during roll call anyway . . .'"

This woman's daughter, middle-aged, her blonde hair pulled back, set her hands on Stella's shoulders, and Stella did the same in return. As they stood there, holding each other, staring at each other for a long silent moment, time seemed to crack open, and Fortunée/Fortunata briefly appeared before us.

Then the moment passed, and she rejoined the other ghosts.

98

"I've been thinking," I say as casually as I can. "I've been wondering . . . won't people who read this story want to know about the young Stella's . . . intimate life. I mean: how it actually began?"

The look she gives me is hard to interpret. There's a touch of mockery in it. That much is clear. Possibly also some exasperation.

"'The young Stella.' You speak of me as if I'm already a character." She pauses. "Which is not so mistaken. Because I am, in a way, even to myself now, after all these years of speaking to you. The young Stella you mention: I know her and I don't know her. I suppose that is how it is when you move so far in time from the person you once were." She pauses again. "But, yes, I will answer your question—in my way."

In her way: Stella is at once an uncanny, and canny, Scheherazade. She knows how to leave me hanging, week to week, moment to moment, sentence to sentence. She has left me hanging, on certain matters, for more than six years now, but I've learned that sometimes it's better not to ask the pressing or follow-up question. It's better, often more interesting, to wait to see what she chooses to tell me, and how.

So I wait.

"The three men I've described to you," she begins gradually, "Luigi, Gennaro, and Renzo, were among the most important people in that period of my life. Each one, you could say, opened a different window for me."

Luigi's influence, she explains, was at first primarily intellectual—he was a teacher, her teacher, after all. Not just in Rhodes, but later, in Florence. What he gave her was incalculable. Literature, history, opera. Friendship. Also he offered her a vision for her life, marriage, a family in Italy, that felt generous and viable—until it didn't.

Renzo was more worldly, cultivated, a man who conducted business all through Europe and the Middle East. His house, his confidence, his ideas, his assuredness, the lively elegant lunches he hosted: all this captivated Stella. What truly impressed her, though in retrospect, was the clarity with which he sized up the situation when the Germans took control of the island. He didn't return home for so much as a change of clothes: he simply headed down to the boats, as she's told me, handed over all his money, and left.

"It's what certain Jews have always done," she says. "The ones who are adept at reading the signs."

But didn't she have any feelings about his leaving without even saying goodbye?

"What I felt was jealousy," she answers unequivocally. "Especially in hindsight, I wish I'd been able to do the same thing."

Then there was Gennaro, the poet/lawyer/soldier, the swimmer with the nineteenth-century sensibility. Of the three of them he was probably the closest to a soul mate Stella had in that period of her life, maybe in her life, period. "I think about him to this day, often. The way he died—which to him felt unavoidable, nonnegotiable, but which to us, at this distance, looks, well, quite different. Yet also the way he lived, and wrote, and spoke. What he gave of himself . . ."

She sits back in her chair and allows a little silence to unfold.

"As you probably realized by now, my intimate life began, yes, with one of these men. It happened. But to specify which one—why do you need to know that?"

She doesn't wait for me to answer—not, when I think of it, that I have an answer.

"It's far more important to understand that I knew these three men and that I knew them, and felt for them, deeply. And that, as a young woman in the Juderia, I saw them, and became friends with them, openly, with my mother's acknowledgment. She never forbade me from going out with them—she met them all, in fact. She had faith in me and she trusted me. She was unusual: she recognized that the world around us was changing and I was changing with it and so, I've come to see, was she.

"Why does it matter who you go to bed with? What was important was the power of these connections. They shaped my life in those years—in truth they helped shape *me*."

99

"We need to finish before I'm finished," Stella emails me early in the new year, when I write to set a date for our first January meeting. "*Dobbiamo finire prima che io finisca*"—with its (to my ear) harsh subjunctive, it feels starker in Italian.

When I arrive on Saturday an uneasy Stella opens the door. Deep shadows wreathe her eyes, and she lowers herself heavily into her customary chair.

I unpack the cookies and apples I bought that morning at the wintry greenmarket at Union Square. I help myself to a glass of water, and I set out my computer and notebook in the usual place on the sofa.

During the week I've forwarded Stella an article about memory in the very old that I read in the *Times*, and we begin here. She tells me she is the same way, forgetting things, trivial things, or why she has walked into one room or another, but with her older memories clearer and clearer. It's not the first time that we have talked about, jointly marveled at, her memory and how it behaves.

"I don't know why it is," she says, "but I see my grandmother sitting there right now on that bench outside our house, the one that was built into the wall and had space for a cushion that she would bring out in the morning and put away again at the end of each day. She is sitting and watching the world go by."

Stella's grandmother, in her advanced age, sits outdoors in bright, balmy Rhodes while Stella, in her advanced age, is cooped up in a New York City apartment in winter.

Stella has described this image to me before, of her grandmother patiently sitting and watching the world go by. She's even shown me this actual bench—has she forgotten? I wonder, as I have in the past when she's repeated herself, whether she's entered that phase of life, the one where the stories are the same, the images are the same, some of the dots no longer connect. Then, as if she's intuiting my thinking, she says, "I've told you before that I didn't actually see my grandmothers die, but I saw them afterward, I saw their bodies. Both of them were eighty-six. They died within a year of each other. And they both looked . . . at peace."

She pauses. "You know, I think there's something reassuring, when you're young, about knowing that people die of old age, just merely of old age. It makes death less . . . less frightening."

Stella falls silent for a moment and then tells me that she has also been thinking a good deal about her parents, about their marriage and how it had been arranged; how her mother, who came from people of significant means—all those banker uncles—married her father, whose background was humbler. The match, on the face of it, seemed unlikely.

"Maybe they were in love," I suggest.

She makes a dismissive sound. Then: "They had great respect for each other. Possibly that, after so many years together, was enough."

For some time Stella and I sit in silence. The cool, pale wintry light seems to have floated in through the windows and thickened around us like a fog. Stella seems faraway, withdrawn.

After a moment she leans forward and turns on one of the white porcelain lamps. The gesture serves as a punctuation mark.

She moves on to something else—or so it seems. She mentions an old *New York Review of Books* she'd come across, in which she'd read a piece by Peter Brooks about a newly reprinted, and reintroduced, collection by Walter Benjamin called *The Storyteller Essays*. She reaches over to the table next to her chair and picks up the magazine. "There's a wonderful line in this article," she says, turning the page and bringing the print closer to her eyes. " 'Death is the sanction of everything the storyteller can relate,' " she reads. " 'It is death that has lent him his authority.' "

The glance she gives me—another punctuation mark—feels like a dart, straight into my chest.

She hands me the magazine; I'm glad not to have to look back at her at just this moment.

My eyes land on a passage. I read it aloud:

> "The Storyteller" stages an opposition of the oral tale to the printed novel. The tale comes to life in the milieu of work and travel and trade: it is an oral transaction in the workshop or with a traveler returned to tell his adventures to those at home. Above all, it involves one living person transmitting experience of life to another in a vital exchange. The personality of the storyteller, Benjamin writes, clings to the story "the way traces of the potter's hand cling to a clay bowl." Stories are compact; they have a "chaste brevity" that precludes explanation. They unfold within the rhythms of work. The tale offers human counsel. What it transmits, in Benjamin's strikingly simple term, is "wisdom."

It's curious, this book, these words, coming along just now.

"You are the traveler," I say to Stella, "and your apartment is our workshop."

She reflects for a moment.

"But have I transmitted wisdom? That is the question."

"*I* believe you have. I *know* you have."

She nods hesitantly, as if not quite convinced.

In the silence that follows I look up at the red and yellow walls, the Turkish rugs on the floor, the rows of tightly packed books, the white lamps sending a wash of light over Stella's long, lined face as they have for more than six years now.

"I had another of those disturbing dreams last night," she says after a pause.

"Oh?"

"I dreamt I was walking toward a light-filled room, and what did I see there but groups of people from Rhodes. I thought, *What are they doing here? Did I invite them?* Rebecca Amato was there, my cousin who wrote that book, and two of my sisters, Renée and Selma. I thought, *Are they calling me, have they come to collect me? Is it my time to join them?*"

"How did it make you feel," I ask, "when you saw them?"

"Puzzled more than anything else. But then . . . then my mother appeared. *That* upset me. And woke me up. It was five in the morning, and I was shaking." She pauses. "It was one of the dreams that continue into your morning, your whole day. You know the kind, the ones that blur the line between your waking life and your dreaming life . . ."

I nod. I know the kind.

Another silence opens up. "I'm curious," I say. "In the dream—what language was everyone speaking? Judeo-Spanish? Italian? English?"

She considers for a moment, then shakes her head.

"I don't know. Dreams . . . dreams are sometimes beyond language. They tell you where you most deeply belong."

"And where is that?"

"With the people who call to you."

100

We need to finish before I'm finished. But Stella's life isn't yet, so neither is her story.

ACKNOWLEDGMENTS

In *One Hundred Saturdays* a life has been offered from memory at a distance of seven, eight, even nine decades from the time in which the events recollected originally took place. The stories themselves have been told in one language, translated into another, then shaped and reshaped as they've found their way onto the page. During the six-plus years that Stella and I met, she revised and revisited her stories more than once; she has, in addition, never stopped taking in new information about the world she was born into, the events she lived through, the central places and people she has known. And over the course of her long life, she has evolved in her thinking about the girl, then the young, and later still the mature, woman she once was, and she is still seeking to understand the person she is today.

I've done my best to explore the factual underpinnings of Stella's recollections. The majority of them appear to line up with the historical record; where there is uncertainty or deviation, I've chosen to stick with Stella, because I've come to trust the emotional and psychological truth of what she has experienced and why she has remembered and chosen to speak about these experiences. Memory is not history; it is one individual human being's grasp, in an individual moment, of what she has lived, and this book is offered with this understanding and in this spirit.

A number of people helped bring *One Hundred Saturdays* into being. Central, of course, is Stella Levi herself. Her candor, rigor, patience, and generosity have taught, and challenged, me profoundly; listening to her and coming to know her has been an unforgettable experience.

Natalia Indrimi, director of the Centro Primo Levi in New York, first introduced me to Stella and has offered indispensable guidance at many junctures; she has also been an insightful and knowledgeable reader. Alessandro Cassin, Centro Primo Levi's deputy director, has been a guardian angel to this project, giving on multiple fronts over many years; he has been an astute reader both of Stella and these pages. To both of them, my deepest gratitude.

Heartfelt thanks to Makena Mezistrano for help with transliterating the Judeo-Spanish following the Aki Yerushalayim system, which represents the language phonetically and was developed by the National Authority for Ladino in Jerusalem. In one consistent variation, the Rhodeslis often employed vowel raising (*mano* becomes *manu*, *borekas* becomes *burekas*, etc.), and where Stella's Judeo-Spanish follows this pattern, so have I. And in certain contexts, where Stella clearly hears, in her memory, a handful of essential words in a particular form, like *enserradura* and *teneme aki*, I have left them thus.

After this note I append an abbreviated list of books and essays about Rhodes and Italy under the Fascist regime that I have mentioned or consulted, but for their willingness to answer numerous questions I would in particular like to thank the scholars Marco Clementi and Anthony McElligott.

For his amazing archival work and generosity, thanks to Aron Hasson.

With her beautiful, vibrant illustrations, Maira Kalman has managed to perceive, and convey, the colorful, spirited atmosphere of prewar Rhodes, and has rendered a sensitive visual analog for certain key moments in the years that followed the deportation.

For various kindnesses and much encouragement, alphabetical thanks as well to Stefano Albertini, Elisabetta Beraldo, Andrea Canobbio, Camuggi Frank, Lucia Frank, Merona Frank, Sophie Frank, Rebecca Samonà, Jo Anne Schlesinger, Ileene Smith, Peter Stasny, Sarah Abrevaya Stein, Jean Strouse, Giorgio van Straten, and Jane Varkell.

Thank you to the John Simon Guggenheim Memorial Foundation for embracing and supporting this project and its author.

And as ever, abundant thanks to my most steadfast readers, Andrea Chapin, Steven Frank, and my agent Sally Wofford-Girand, and to the perspicacious and enthusiastic Lauren Wein, who along with Amy Guay and the rest of the team at Avid Reader Press, have given *One Hundred Saturdays* such a splendid home.

Alhadeff, Vittorio. *Le chêne de Rhodes: Saga d'une grande famille sépharde.* Paris: Lior éditions, 2019.

Angel, Marc D. *The Jews of Rhodes: The History of a Sephardic Community.* New York: Sepher-Hermon Press, 1998.

Benatar, Isaac. *Rhodes and the Holocaust: The Story of the Jewish Community from the Mediterranean Island of Rhodes.* Bloomington, IN: iUniverse, 2010.

Benatar, Jacqueline, and Myriam Benatar. *Si je t'oublie, Rhodes: Mémorial de la Communauté juive de Rhodes de 1939 à 1945.* Jerusalem: Editions JEM et Erez, 2012; Correctum et Addendum, 2019.

Bierman, John. *Odyssey: The Last Great Escape from Nazi-Dominated Europe.* New York: Simon and Schuster, 1984.

Clementi, Marco, and Eirini Toliou. *Gli ultimi ebrei di Rodi: Leggi razziali e deportazioni nel Dodecaneso italiano (1938–1948).* Rome: DeriveApprodi, 2015.

Franco, Hizkia M. *The Jewish Martyrs of Rhodes and Cos.* New York: HarperCollins, 1994.

Galante, Avram. *Histoire des juifs de Turquie.* Vol. 7. Istanbul: Isis Press, 1988.

Levi, Primo. *The Complete Works of Primo Levi.* Edited by Ann Goldstein. New York: Liveright, 2015.

Levis Sullam, Simon. *The Italian Executioners: The Genocide of the Jews of Italy.* Princeton, NJ: Princeton University Press, 2018.

Lévy, Isaac Jack. *Jewish Rhodes: A Lost Culture.* Berkeley, CA: Judah L. Magnes Museum, 1989.

———, and Rosemary Lévy Zumwalt. *Ritual Medical Lore of Sephardic Women: Sweetening the Spirits, Healing the Sick.* Urbana and Chicago: University of Illinois Press, 2022.

Levy, Rebecca Amato. *I Remember Rhodes.* New York: Sepher-Hermon Press, 1987.

Livingston, Michael A. *The Fascists and the Jews of Italy: Mussolini's Race Laws, 1938–1943.* Cambridge, UK: Cambridge University Press, 2014.

McElligott, Anthony. "The Deportation of the Jews of Rhodes, 1944: An Integrated History." In *The Holocaust in Greece*, edited by Giorgos Antoniou and A. Dirk Moses, 58–85. Cambridge, UK: Cambridge University Press, 2018.

Menascé, Esther Fintz. *Gli ebrei a Rodi: Storia di un'antica comunità annietata dai nazisti.* Milan: Guerini e Associati, 1992.

———. *A History of Jewish Rhodes.* Los Angeles: Rhodes Jewish Historical Foundation, 2014.

Modiano, Sami. *Per questo ho vissuto: La mia vita ad Auschwitz-Birkenau e altri esili.* Milan: RCS Libri, 2013.

Pignataro, Luca. *Il Dodecaneso italiano 1912–1947.* Vol. 3. Chieti, IT: Edizioni Solfanelli, 2018.

Sarfatti, Michele. *The Jews in Mussolini's Italy: From Equality to Persecution.* Madison: University of Wisconsin Press, 2006.

———. *La Shoah in Italia: La persecuzione degli ebrei sotto il fascismo.* Torino, IT: Giulio Einaudi Editore, 2005.

Shachar, Nathan. *The Lost Worlds of Rhodes: Greeks, Italians, Jews and Turks Between Tradition and Modernity.* Eastbourne, UK: Sussex Academic Press, 2013.

Stille, Alexander. *Benevolence and Betrayal: Five Italian Jewish Families Under Fascism.* New York: Summit Books, 1991.

Tescione, Gennaro. *Una luce che si spense il 9 dicembre 1943.* Caserta, IT: Società di Storia Patria di Terra di Lavoro, 1993.

Varon, Laura. *The Juderia: A Holocaust Survivor's Tribute to the Jewish Community of Rhodes.* Westport, CT: Praeger, 1999.

ABOUT THE AUTHOR

MICHAEL FRANK is the author of *What Is Missing,* a novel, and *The Mighty Franks,* a memoir, which was awarded the 2018 JQ Wingate Prize and was named one of the best books of the year by *The Telegraph* and *The New Statesman.* The recipient of a 2020 Guggenheim Fellowship, he lives with his family in New York City and Camogli, Italy.

ABOUT THE ILLUSTRATOR

MAIRA KALMAN is the author/illustrator of more than thirty books for adults and children and a contributor to *The New Yorker* and the *New York Times.* She lives in New York City.